The Meaning of Life

The Meaning of Life

Steve Pavlina

WAKING LION PRESS

ISBN 978-1-4341-0564-6

Published by Waking Lion Press, an imprint of the Editorium

Waking Lion Press™ and Editorium™ are trademarks of:

The Editorium, LLC
West Jordan, UT 84081-6132
www.editorium.com

Contents

Chapter 1

The Meaning of Life

What is the meaning of life? Why are we here? Is there a God or isn't there, and if there is a God, what is its nature? Of all the world's religions, which one is the most correct? Is there an afterlife? Are we primarily physical beings or spiritual beings?

People have struggled for millennia to tackle these questions. Wars have been fought over them. But as much as these questions cause people to lose their heads (sometimes figuratively, sometimes literally), the bottom line is that these are very practical questions.

Behind the Wheel

The way we answer these questions will provide the ultimate context for everything else we do with our lives. If we place any value on our lives at all, we must give some consideration to these questions.

Let's say you have your life organized around goals, projects, and actions. You set a goal like starting a new internet business. You break it down into projects like writing a business plan and launching your web site. And then you break those projects down into actions like going to the bank to open a business account and registering your domain name. Fair enough.

But why start the business in the first place? What's the point? Why pick this goal vs. any other goal? Why even set goals at all?

What determines the goals you set (or don't set) is your context. Your context is your collection of beliefs and values. So if the values of money and freedom are part of your context, you might be inclined to set a goal to start a new business. But with different kinds of values — a different context — you may be disinclined to set goals at all.

The most significant part of your context is your collection of beliefs about the nature of reality, which includes your religious, spiritual, and philosophical beliefs. Your overall beliefs about the universe will largely determine your results. Context dictates goals. Goals dictate projects. Projects dictate actions. Actions dictate results.

Within a certain context, it will be virtually impossible for you to achieve certain results because you'll never set the required goals that will lead to those results.

Your context works like a filter. When you are inside a particular context, you lose access to the potential goals, projects, and actions that lie outside that context. For example, if your context includes the belief that criminal behavior is very bad, then you aren't likely to work towards becoming a future leader in organized crime.

Walking in My Shoes

This is a *long* personal story, but I think you'll find it interesting. If you take the time to read it, I want you to notice how my beliefs (my context) shifted over time and how dramatically they changed my results.

For half of my life, I've been searching for the context that would give me the best possible life. Of course, this is a strange pursuit because it requires searching for a context while at the same time always being stuck inside of one. In other words, the definition of "best possible life" is also part of any context, so I have to find a context that both defines that term *and* provides a means to fulfill it.

This pursuit began almost accidentally for me, but eventually I began pursuing it consciously.

Halo

For the first half of my life, until the age of 17, I was Catholic/Christian, baptized and confirmed. I went through eight years of Catholic grammar school followed by four years of Catholic high school. I was a boy scout for several years and earned the Ad Altare Dei award. I prayed every day and accepted all that I was taught as true. I went to Church every Sunday with my family. All of my friends and family were Christian, so I knew nothing of other belief systems. My father was an altar boy when he was young, and his brother (my uncle) is a Catholic priest. One of my cousins is a member of Campus Crusade for Christ. In high school I went to optional religious retreats and did community service, both at a convalescent home and at a preschool for children with disabilities. I expected to be Catholic for life.

Blasphemous Rumors

But near the end of my junior year of high school, I went through an experience that I'd have to describe as an awakening. It was as if a new part of my brain suddenly switched on, popping me into a higher state of awareness. Perhaps it was just a side effect of the maturation process. I began to openly question the beliefs that had been conditioned into me since childhood. Blind acceptance of what I was taught wasn't enough for me anymore. I wanted to go behind the scenes, uproot any incongruencies, and see if these beliefs actually made sense to me. I started raising a lot of questions but found few people would honestly discuss them. Most simply dismissed me or became defensive. But I was intensely curious, not hostile about it. My family was closed to discussing the whole thing, but I did find a few open-minded teachers. My high school (Loyola High in Los Angeles) was a Jesuit school, and the Jesuits are very liberal as far as priests go.

I was disappointed though. What I found was that regardless of their education and their much greater life experience, very few of my friends and teachers ever bothered to question their beliefs openly. And that really gave me a huge shot of doubt. I thought, "If everyone is just accepting all of this blindly and no one is even questioning it, why should I believe it?" Over a period of months the doubt only grew stronger, and I transferred more of my faith from my Catholic upbringing to my own intelligence and senses. Eventually I just dropped the whole context entirely, and in the absence of any other viable contexts to choose from, I became an atheist.

I entered my senior year of Catholic high school as a 17-year old atheist. Oh, the irony. Initially I wasn't sure what to expect, but soon I found the context of atheism to be incredibly empowering. Having shed all my old beliefs, I felt like my brain had gotten an intelligence upgrade. I could think so much more clearly, and my mind seemed to work much better. I also felt more in control of my life than ever before. Without a belief in God, I assumed total responsibility for my results in life. School was easier than ever for me, even though I was taking all the school's most challenging classes, most of them AP courses. I was so good at calculus that my teacher actually gave me a special test, different from the rest of the class. And one time my AP physics teacher came to me before school to have me show him how to solve a difficult physics problem. I especially found math and science classes so easy that I began looking for new ways to challenge myself. So I'd try to do my entire homework assignment on a 1 by 1 square of paper, or I'd do it in crayon on the back of a cereal box cover, or I'd color in my polar graphs with colored pencil and turn it into artwork. People thought I was wacky, but I mainly did these things to keep it interesting because the problems themselves posed no challenge. You haven't really lived until you've done calculus in crayon.

I made no secret of the fact that I was an atheist, so when taking religion classes, I'd regurgitate all the raw data needed to ace a test, but whenever there were open-ended essay questions, I'd address them from an atheistic perspective. I'm grateful the Jesuits were as liberal as they were and tolerated my behavior. I have to give them a lot of credit for that.

My family was not happy about all this, especially when my subscription to American Atheist magazine started coming in the mail (I got good at intercepting the mail early). But I was doing so well in school that it was hard for them to complain, and they didn't want to openly address any of my questions, even though I'd have been happy to do so. They did force me to keep going to church though, which I tolerated for a while because I knew I'd be moving out in a year anyway. But eventually I started sitting in a different part of the church and would sneak out the back and go for a walk and return just before it ended. But one time the mass ended earlier than expected, and I got back too late. My family was already at the car and saw me walking down the street. Whoops! They drove off without me. But instead of walking the two miles home, I stayed out the entire day and didn't return until midnight. Aside from weddings and funerals, that was the last time I ever went to church.

Despite these conflicts, my senior year in high school was by far my best ever. I aced all my classes and was accepted into six colleges as a computer science major: Cal Tech, UCLA (partial scholarship), UC San Diego (full scholarship), UC Berkeley, Carnegie Mellon, and Harvey Mudd.

I opted to go to UC Berkeley because at the time, its computer science program was the highest rated in the country. I was very happy to move out and finally be on my own. In the fall of 1989 I moved to Berkeley and lived in the freshman dorms.

Then things got weird.

Judas

While at Berkeley my atheism context was further molded. No longer surrounded by Catholics, I met a lot of interesting people there with a wide variety of belief systems. I quickly made a lot of new friends who were very intelligent, and some were open to discussing the nature of reality. I think my Catholic upbringing was like a coiled spring — as soon as I left behind the environment that kept the spring coiled, I immediately shot to the other end of the spectrum. But I went way too far with it. I not only shed my old religious beliefs, but along with it went my whole concept of morality. I was like the guy in Mark Twain's short story "The Facts Concerning the Recent Carnival of Crime in Connecticut," a story about a guy who kills his conscience.

I started embracing all the stuff that was basically the opposite of my upbringing. I completely lost all interest in school and hardly ever went to class. I really didn't care at all about getting my degree. I went to parties almost every week and drank a lot, one time doing about 14 drinks in a row and waking up with no memory of how I got to bed. I had to ask friends to piece together pieces of the previous night. To this day I'm certain I drank more alcohol before the age of 21 than after (and I'm 34 now).

I also started shoplifting — a lot. The first time I did it simply because it was something I'd never done before, something I could never do as a Catholic. It was like a task to be marked off a checklist. But I soon became addicted to the emotional high of it, and I kept doing it more and more, eventually to the point of doing it several times a day.

I virtually never stole stuff to keep it. I'd give away most of what I stole to other people, or I'd just throw it in the trash afterwards. About a month into my first semester, I got arrested. 4 months probation. I took about a week off and went right back to it, although I became a bit more cautious about it. One week after the probation period ended, I got arrested again and ended up with 40 hours of community service. I did the service, and soon went right back into stealing. But I refined my methods even more, making it much harder for me to get caught. A few close calls only gave me more confidence.

I grew so accustomed to this behavior that I could steal without my heart skipping a beat. No fear. So I had to keep upping the dosage. At first I started setting little goals, like seeing how many large candy bars I could fit in my pockets at once (13), or trying to steal every bottle of white out from the student store in one day (over 50 bottles). Then I just gave away all the candy and white out to fellow students.

I wasn't doing well in school and was put on academic probation too. They do that when you don't show up to class. I can't say I really cared much though.

But things went from bad to worse when I met another student who was about as morally corrupted as I was, and we became fast friends. I stopped doing the (risky) shoplifting, and together we planned and implemented a two-person theft where the odds of getting caught were very low. It worked again and again, and we both started making some actual money from it. To play it safe and not keep hitting the same locations over and over, we expanded our circle to go way beyond Berkeley to an almost 100-mile radius, from San Francisco to Sacramento to Fresno. Over a period of about a year, we gradually escalated each theft to a dollar value that was now well into the grand theft range (at the time any theft above $400). I think our weekend record was about $2400 worth of stuff.

Shouldn't Have Done That

Eventually I got caught again, this time for grand theft. Not good. Before this arrest I had discovered that because of my priors, I'd be looking at about two years in jail if I got convicted of grand theft. Not good at all.

And to make it even worse, I was arrested in Sacramento, about a 2-hour drive from Berkeley. But my partner couldn't wait around and expose himself too, so he drove back. I was stuck sitting in the county jail for an ID hold. I never stole with ID on me, and I gave the police one of my many fake names, but they of course didn't take my word for it, so I had to wait in a cell while they ran my fingerprints trying to figure out who I was.

So there I was . . . 19 years old, sitting in jail on Superbowl Sunday 1991. Expecting that I was about to lose my freedom for the next two years.

THUNK!

That was the sound of reality crashing down around me. For the first several hours, I was in shock, unable to think straight. Maybe it was the orange clothes. But with nothing to do but sit and think for an indefinite period of time, I started asking all the big questions again. What the hell was I doing here? Was this really me?

But now my answers were very different. I realized that this context was all wrong. I resigned myself to the fact that I'd have to spend the next couple years in jail, but I also knew that I had changed permanently and that this way of life had now ended. Two years in jail . . . this would be a painful lesson. But at least I had learned it. I didn't have a complete replacement context yet, but I began to plant the seed of one. That seed was the realization that no matter how bad things seemed, in the future they could be better. I knew I would eventually recover and rebound. It might be a number of years before I was back on my feet again, but I knew with certainty that I could survive it. Although I wouldn't have labeled it as such at the time, this was the moment when the idea of personal growth got planted in me. It was the idea that no matter how bad things are right now, I still have the capacity to grow through them and to emerge in a better position in the future. That idea was all I had, but it was enough to allow me to cope.

Three days later I was released. They'd succeeded in identifying me. I was given a court date and sent on my way, charged with felony grand theft. It was around sunset. At first I walked around the Capitol building and garden in Sacramento, just enjoying the fresh air and happy that I'd at least have a few more months of freedom. Jail is extremely boring, and I was just in the county jail, not prison. Unfortunately I had a more immediate problem to deal with. I had no ID, only $18 cash on me, and I had to find a way to go 120 miles to get back home. As luck would have it, I was able to take a late night bus to Oakland for only $16, and from there my (ex) partner gave me a ride home.

Upon returning to my apartment, I found in the mail a letter from UC Berkeley stating that I was expelled. They do that when your GPA starts with the decimal point.

A Broken Frame

For the next few months while waiting for my court date, I was in a bit of a funk. I didn't do much of anything at all. I slept a lot, took long walks, and played a lot of video games. It's hard to set goals when you expect to be going to jail for a while.

Eventually I got a lawyer and met with him to discuss my case. Before I could open my mouth, he said, "Well, I've reviewed your case, and since this is your first offense, I'm pretty sure we can get it reduced to petty theft, so you'd only end up with some community service if we plead no contest. I'm on great terms with the D.A., so I'm pretty sure he'll go for it. I strongly advise against going to trial, as the evidence against you is overwhelming, seeing as you were caught red handed." First offense? Huh? Immediately my brain filled with thoughts like, "Why does he think this is my first offense? Doesn't he know about my priors? And if he thinks this is a first offense, will the rest of the court also think it's a first offense? Should I correct my lawyer on this oversight?" After mulling it over in my mind for a few seconds, I decided I'd damn well better keep my mouth shut. It might backfire on me, but there was a chance that it might frontfire too. I figured that worst case, I'd have an angry lawyer to deal with. But the best case was too good to pass up. Grand theft was a felony; petty theft was only a misdemeanor. I had to take the risk. Of course, taking risks was something all too familiar for me.

Several weeks later we went to court. My plan was to keep my mouth shut as much as possible and only say the absolute minimum. Outside the courtroom I reviewed the court's basic info about the case. They had indeed connected me with my real identity, but they also had my fake name listed too. No priors were listed. My best guess is that someone screwed up and searched for priors based on my fake name instead of my real name, even though the case was going to court under my real name. Human error? Computer error? Who knows? But one big error either way.

Sure enough when we got into the courtroom (a place that was becoming increasingly familiar), the court remained under the assumption that this was a first offense and processed it as such. I pleaded no contest to the reduced charge of petty theft and got 60 hours community service. I did those 60 hours like it was a dream job, knowing that it could have been 17,520 hours.

My head was spinning. What had just happened? The next two years were now mine again.

Construction Time Again

Soon I moved back to L.A. and got a nothing retail sales job for $6 an hour and took a few nothing classes on the side. I'd had quite enough excitement over the past couple years, and I just wanted to enjoy a quiet normal life for a while . . . spend some time below the radar. I reconnected with old high school friends who were going to UCLA and hung out at their fraternity house at times, but I usually stayed clear of the parties. I played a lot of frisbee golf, tennis, and computer games (especially the Sierra adventure games which were popular in the early 90s). I tried to keep life very simple. I spent a lot of time analyzing my experience at Berkeley, needing to understand it so as to be able to prevent myself from ever going down that path again. But I kept my thoughts about all this to myself.

I knew I had a lot of personal rebuilding to do, but I also

knew that I couldn't go backwards. The morals and beliefs by which I was raised were broken, but living without a sense of conscience clearly wasn't an option. Was a belief in God required to live by a code of ethics?

I became aware that despite how negative my experiences seemed, they forever changed me in a good way too. By going through those experiences, I had unlocked access to a part of myself that was previously dormant — my courage. Although I had done things that were very foolish, they also took a lot of courage to do. I learned to act in spite of fear again and again. And this conditioning stayed with me. Because I had already faced the prospect of going to jail, any failure that would have a lesser negative consequence than jail wouldn't phase me. To this day fear of failure has very little power over me. I just say to myself, "Hey, if it's not going to land me in jail, how bad could it be?"

Of course I had to learn how to temper this courage with some sense of morality and common sense. So during this year of quiet reflection, I gradually shifted my context to create a new personal code of ethics to guide me. But instead of being rooted in religion, I built it in a more humanistic manner, integrating values like honor, honesty, integrity, humility, and fairness. It was a very deliberate and conscious rebuilding process that would continue for at least a few more years. But even during this time of 1991–92 as I was just beginning, it gave me some stability and gradually became my most empowering context up to that point. It didn't take me long to realize that the courage I had developed could become a powerful asset for me if I learned how to use it intelligently.

I was ready for a new challenge.

Nothing to Fear

In the Fall of 1992, I decided to go back to college, starting over as a freshman. This time I went to Cal State University, Northridge (CSUN). The computer science program wasn't impacted, so all I had to do to get accepted was to apply. I moved into the dorms at age 21. But I was no longer the same person I was at 18. I was still an atheist religiously, but now I had a strong collection of personal values to guide me. I wanted to see what I was capable of and what these new values might do for me, especially the value of integrity. There would be no cheating, no stealing, no drinking. For me it was all about setting goals and taking action and pushing myself to do my best. My courage was like a new power source, but now I had a strong harness on it. My Berkeley friends had said to me, "If you'd put all the energy you put into criminal behavior into your studies, you'd get straight As."

But I knew I could get straight As. I'd done that in high school taking all honors classes. That wasn't a big enough challenge. So I upped the bar my first semester, opting to take 31 units (10 classes). The average student takes 12–15 units per semester. Unfortunately the dean of the computer science department wouldn't approve my extra units. She was the gatekeeper, and she thought I was either joking or nuts. I talked her up from 18 units to 25 units, but there she stood firm, and even then she still thought I was probably joking. So I took 25 units at CSUN and enrolled in another six units off campus, for a total of 31 units. That was against the rules, since the extra unit approval was technically inclusive of off-campus units too, but I wasn't going to let pointless bureaucracy stop me.

I devoted myself to the study of time management and learned to use my time very efficiently. I aced all my classes and took my straight-A report cards from both schools back to the dean, now asking for 39 units for my second semester. This time it wasn't hard to get her approval, but I think she was a bit scared of me when I left. I aced that semester too. Then in the summer of 1993 I did full-time contract work as a game programmer and also went vegetarian. No summer school. In my third and final semester, I added a double major in mathematics (which was pretty easy to get, since there were so many courses in common with computer science), and I took 37 units while continuing to work full-time. I graduated with a 3.94 GPA and ended up receiving an award for the top computer science student each year. Two degrees in three semesters.

This experience gave me a deeper appreciation of the power of context. I would not have even attempted such a thing as a Catholic. I would never have set the goals I did. I'm not sure anyone can truly understand how different reality seems from the perspective of different contexts if you've never switched contexts. If you subscribe to a disempowering context, you may be absolutely crippled in your ability to effectively tackle certain challenges no matter how hard you try (if you even try at all).

In the year after graduation, I started Dexterity Software, met my future wife, and continued to explore different belief systems. But now I was doing it very consciously. I was driven by the idea that if one context could open the door to previously untapped potential, then what could other contexts do? Might there be a better context than my current one? My experiences at Berkeley and CSUN were totally opposite, and I knew it was because of my different belief systems. One "religion" nearly sent me to prison; the other allowed me to successfully tap into potential I never knew was within me. I absolutely had to learn more about this.

Over the next decade I experimented with agnosticism, various new-agey belief systems, Buddhism, objectivism, and more. I even tried Scientology for a few months just to see what it was like. I wanted to assimilate a variety of different contexts, experience them from the inside, and then back off and compare their strengths and weaknesses. This produced a lot of instability in my life but also tremendous growth.

I was like a chef trying different ingredients to discover what recipe of beliefs would lead to the best life. And again, the definition of "best" is part of the recipe itself, so my understanding of the meaning of life was also in flux.

Many times I found that a new context set me back, and my results began to decline. Other times my new context was more empowering, and I again started to surge ahead. In the long run as I integrated new empowering beliefs and shed disempowering ones, my life began to improve across the board. For the past year they've been fairly stable, and this has by far been my best year ever.

Flexible

Our beliefs act as lenses. These lenses can help us see things we can't otherwise see, but they can also block us from seeing parts of reality. I see a huge part of personal development as the study of these lenses — these belief systems. There are an infinite number of lenses, so the quest never ends, but the more lenses you examine personally, the more you understand about the nature of reality and your role within it.

I have not experienced any organized belief system that is

not disempowering in some way. The problem is that they all have a fixed perspective. If you look at reality from any single perspective, you are only perceiving the projection of reality onto your belief system, not reality itself. The more rigid your perspective, the more detail you miss (detail which doesn't fall upon your projection but does fall upon others), and the less of your true potential you're able to tap.

For several years I would have described my religion as a field and not a fixed point. It was multi-contextual. I kept the context floating and tried to see reality from multiple perspectives. At first this was unsettling and made it hard to set goals and take action, but I found it worthwhile because it gave me much greater clarity. I began seeing patterns in where certain perspectives would lead, both for myself and others. Just as you might imagine where a life of crime will ultimately lead, you can also gain a subtler understanding of where a belief in a certain type of God will lead and how that path compares to other choices. This is complicated because we aren't dealing with fixed points for either the starting point or the destination. It's about fields of possibility leading to fields of potential. For example, a life of crime can begin and end in many ways, but you can still see some general patterns in the pathways from start to finish. You can make some generalizations that will be fairly accurate.

As a result of this introspection, I was able to shed certain beliefs and strengthen others. Some beliefs I found consistently disempowering, meaning that if I adopted them, I would be denying myself access to valuable potential. These included the belief in heaven/hell and the belief in a higher power. That second one may seem surprising, but I opted to let it go because I consistently found it less empowering than a belief in a lower power. An example of a higher power would be a consciously aware God or gods such as found in Christianity or Greek mythology. A lower power would be like a field that is able to respond to your intentions, sort of like "the force" in Star Wars or what some people refer to as "source." You can pray to either type of power, but in the first case you're asking, and in the second case, you're declaring. Many people, myself included, have noted that declarative prayer works better than no prayer and better than asking prayer. I see it mainly as putting out an intention.

So in deciding which beliefs to embrace and which to drop, I keep going back to the concepts of empowerment and potential. I strive to dump beliefs that curtail my ability to access my potential while strengthening beliefs that unlock more potential. If one form of prayer doesn't seem to work at all, but another one works often, I'm going to adopt more of the latter context.

World in My Eyes

My overall religion has effectively become *a religion of personal growth*. Every year I continue to tweak my beliefs to try to bring them into closer alignment with my best understanding of how reality actually works. The better we understand reality, the more potential we unlock. Just as understanding a new law of physics can allow us to do things we could never previously do, beliefs about reality work the same way. If you're stuck with a belief in a flat earth, it's going to limit your potential actions and results. Similarly, if your religious beliefs are too great a mismatch for actual reality, you'll be doomed to spend your life only tapping a fraction of your true potential. In my "religion," knowingly leaving my potential untapped is sinful. Personal optimization is deeply embedded into my sense of morality. Not growing is morally wrong to me — it runs contrary to my understanding of the purpose of life.

The only reliable means I've found for discovering what beliefs are empowering is to test them and compare them to other beliefs. This is something I initially fell into unconsciously and in a very destructive manner. But when done consciously and intelligently, it can give you a whole new perspective on life. Just as people who travel a lot report being changed by their experiences of other cultures, you can also expect to be changed by experiencing different belief systems.

I don't expect everyone else to subscribe to my religion of course. It was a very personal choice of mine and has been undoubtedly shaped by my unique experiences. Yet choosing my beliefs consciously has allowed me access to parts of my potential that I'd never have been able to tap with other belief systems. In most cases I'd have been stuck being way too passive and would have failed to push myself. I'd have been more inclined to accept my given lot in life instead of consciously co-creating it. Because my religion is based on working actively on my personal growth and helping others to do the same, I am driven to take action. Good thoughts or intentions aren't enough.

Another part of my religion is to strive to become the best me I can become, not a copy of Jesus or Buddha or anyone else. This means spending a lot of time learning about my own strengths and weaknesses and figuring out where I can grow and what I may have to simply accept.

Everything Counts

Do your current beliefs empower you to be your best, or do they doom you to live as a mere shadow of what you could be? Can you honestly say that you are doing your best or very close to it? Are you living congruently with your most deeply held beliefs? Whatever your religious or spiritual beliefs, how well do you practice them? Do you walk your talk?

On Monday as I walked around the Las Vegas Strip, I saw a downtrodden homeless man sitting on one of the overhead walkways asking for money. As over a hundred people passed by him each minute, no one even stopped to give him a kind word or a smile. I thought to myself, "Where are all the Christians?" If Jesus is the model for Christian behavior, what would Jesus do in that situation? What would other role models do? What would you do?

By their words I hear that most Americans are Christian. By their actions I see that most aren't.

If you really believe something, you will act in accordance with that belief — always. If you believe in gravity, you will never attempt to defy it. If you claim to hold a belief but act incongruently, then you don't actually believe it. You're only kidding yourself. Casual faith isn't.

Actions, not words, reveal beliefs. If you want to understand what you truly believe, observe your actions. This may take some courage to do, but if you follow the trail of your actions, it will lead you to a more congruent belief system. And once there you can begin consciously moving towards new beliefs that empower you, while your actions and beliefs remain congruent along the way. But you'll make no progress as long as you claim to believe one thing but consistently act in violation of it. Most people in such a situation will spend time trying to get their actions to better reflect their so-called beliefs . . . and meet with nothing but frustration. I say first get your beliefs in line with your actions and reach the point of being totally honest with yourself, doubts and all. Then you'll find it far easier to move forward. Don't be afraid to do this — no divine being is going to smite you for being honest with yourself. And if one ever happens to show up, you always have me to use as a scapegoat.

Although it can be a bumpy ride (it certainly was for me), you'll come out the other end a far more integrated and empowered human being. Internal incongruencies absolutely cripple us, forcing us to live on only a fraction of our potential. When our actions and beliefs are in conflict, we can't think as well. We become less intelligent and less resourceful — easily manipulated by others. We have no clarity at all, and we can't seem to get moving in a consistent direction. We're like a rudderless ship, being tossed around by the waves.

Congruency is clarity. When you get clear about what you truly believe about reality by observing your actions and admitting the deepest, darkest truths to yourself that you never wanted to face, you'll set yourself on a path of growth that will put all your earlier accomplishments to shame. You'll unlock access to resources that were previously dormant — greater intelligence, greater awareness, greater conscience. And you'll finally start living up to the greatness that has been too long buried under a pile of denial.

Don't be afraid to face who you really are. You're a lot stronger than you realize.

Chapter 2

How Shall We Live?

How shall we live? What shall we live for, if anything? How can we decide right from wrong? Is there any reasonable way to answer these questions that doesn't require us to fall back on blind faith?

Let's Ask the Old Greeks

People have been striving to answer these questions literally for thousands of years. One who attempted it was Socrates (469–399 BC). One of his most powerful breakthroughs was the idea of scrutinizing one's beliefs through a type of cross-examination which became known as the dialectic. This involved asking and answering probing questions in order to arrive at something that could be considered true. Essentially he played devil's advocate and challenged people to justify what they claimed to know.

For example, there's a story where Socrates met a young man who was going to court to charge his father with impiety. When Socrates learned of this, he acknowledged the man as a presumed expert in piety, stating that one must be an expert in piety in order to charge his own father with impiety. Then Socrates humbly asked the man to define piety for him, a concept of which Socrates claimed ignorance. The man repeatedly tried in vain to define it, with Socrates offering a simple and undeniable explanation why each answer offered couldn't be valid. It's easy to see that Socrates would ultimately piss off the establishment and get himself sentenced to death. He could have escaped, but he chose to stay in Athens and take the poison. Socrates had tremendous respect for the law, even when it meant sacrificing his life to remain true to his principles. As I read about his life, I couldn't help but develop a tremendous respect for him and his philosophy of life.

Another philosopher who made a significant dent in the question of how to live was Aristotle (384–322 BC), who studied under Plato (Plato studied under Socrates). A young Aristotle expanded on Plato's ideas regarding the nature of reality (the world of forms), but eventually Aristotle began moving in a new direction and tackled the problem of how one should live.

Aristotle's best answer for how one should live was the concept of *eudaimonia*. Unfortunately this word has been tough to translate to English, so there are two favored translations I'm aware of. The first is "happiness," and the second is "human flourishing." Most other translations I've seen are variations on one of these. Personally I might translate this term as "fulfillment," although that's not perfectly accurate either. Eudaimonia is a process of living virtuously, not a fixed state of being. It's not really an emotion like "happiness" suggests. Aristotle came up with this answer because he found that eudaimonia was the only potential goal of life that could be considered an end in itself rather than a means to another end. I think this is the reason that happiness is perhaps the most popular translation because happiness is an end in itself, not a means to anything else.

Aristotle was interested in finding a right way to live, if such a thing could be said to exist. His answer of eudaimonia consists of two main components: virtuous action and contemplation. The main problem is that the means to discover the virtues was to look at people who seemed to be flourishing and living virtuously and take note of how they lived. As it turned out, such people would usually behave with some degree of integrity, honor, courage, honesty, rationality, fairness, etc. This is not merely an internal observation that one assesses in oneself — such values can be witnessed from the outside in, so Aristotle makes some progress here in attempting to create a semi-objective standard for right living. Like Socrates, Aristotle was also sentenced to death, but he chose to flee Athens and live in exile. (I tell you I'm immensely grateful to live in a society where philosophizing doesn't currently carry the death penalty.)

The main problem I see in Aristotle's insightful attempt to answer this question is that his solution is somewhat circular. In order to live well, we need to live virtuously and spend time on self-reflection and study, but how do we know what criteria to use in selecting the virtues or in choosing what to study? We basically have to find people that seem to be living well and flourishing — or in Aristotle's time, it was suggested that we might also strive to emulate the gods, since they certainly seemed to be doing well. This isn't unlike certain religions today that provide a model of virtue to attempt to emulate. Aristotle doesn't answer one key question though: What is the best life one could possibly live? Eudaimonia suggests a way to go about finding the answer to this question, but it still leaves some gaping holes.

After Aristotle many others addressed the question of how to live. Every religion has its own answer. Some people say there's no answer, that the answer doesn't matter, that the answer is impossible for us to know, or that the answer is purely a matter of personal choice. The worst answer of all though is what most people do — to ignore the question entirely.

Choosing Your Own Context

What should you live for? Wealth? Power? Service? Longevity? Reason? Love? Faith? Family? God? Virtue? Happiness? Fulfillment? Comfort? Contentment? Integrity? There are hundreds of values to choose from.

It is important to make a global choice about how to live our lives, since this decision sets the context for everything else we do. If you don't choose your context, you get the default/average context, which means you're essentially letting others dictate your context. To make a gross generalization, in the USA this is a largely commercial/materialist context. It says to get a job, have a family, save some money, and retire. Be a good citizen and don't get into too much trouble. But don't really matter either. Be a good cog. Other cultures have their own default contexts. Most people simply subscribe to the default context of their culture with minor individual variations.

Sticking to your culture's default context is among the worst of your options. Let's consider the simple cases of a democracy vs. a dictatorship. In a democracy no one is really in charge of the cultural context as a whole, so the most common contexts end up as a mish-mash of bits and pieces that lack overall congruency. This will generally lead to confusion and mediocrity. Such a society will only provide a very fuzzy notion of how you should live, like getting a job, having a family, staying out of trouble, and retiring quietly. Ask an American what it means to live the best possible life, and you'll get a lot of different answers, and most of them will be fairly fuzzy and unfocused — the kinds of answers that Socrates would shoot full of holes.

Now if you happen to live under a culture where the context is consciously directed, then you have to worry about who's directing it and what their motives are and whether or not you can trust them. Where you find a strong dictatorship, you'll usually see a more focused context than in a democracy. If you were to have asked someone from Nazi Germany what it means to live the best possible life, I'd bet the answers would have been more homogeneous and focused. But the problem of course is that such contexts are often designed to keep the context maintainers in power. There's more pressure to conform to such a context. In the long run this type of context will usually lead to disillusionment, numbness, or fanaticism.

So if you let society dictate your context (which is what will happen by default in the absence of conscious choice), you'll most likely wind up with a very fuzzy and unfocused context or one that's focused on the wrong spot. Not a great choice either way. Certainly not the optimal choice. Such a context won't provide you with enough guidance for how to live properly. You'll spend a lot of time guessing your way through life or making a lot of mistakes that come back to haunt you later.

Ultimately if you want to get closer to the "best possible life" for you, you have to pick your own context. You can't merely inherit the default context of your society and live up to what others expect of you. If you try to conform, you're going to waste your life compared to what you might have done with it if you chose a better context.

So how the heck are we supposed to figure out how to live? Do we simply guess and hope for the best? Is there any rational, sane way to make such a hefty decision?

I can't make this decision for you, but I can explain how I made this decision for myself, ultimately providing me with an answer that I found very satisfying. I think part of my answer is personal, but I also see part of it as being universal to all of us.

Living the Virtues

After I reached adulthood and began seriously pondering the question of how to live, the first major stopping point was essentially where Aristotle left off. In my early and mid-20s, I spent a lot of time working on living virtuously. I saw living the best possible life as becoming a person of virtue: to live with honor, integrity, courage, compassion, etc. I listed out the virtues I wanted to attain and even set about inventing exercises to help myself develop them. Benjamin Franklin did something very similar, as I read in his autobiography, and each week he chose to focus on one particular virtue in order to develop his character.

Oddly, there was a particular computer game I absolutely fell in love with during this time — *Ultima IV*. To date I would have to say it is still my favorite game of all time. In this role-playing game you are the Avatar, a seeker of truth, and your goal is not to destroy some enemy but rather to attain what is called the Codex of Ultimate Wisdom. In order to achieve this goal, you must develop your character in the eight virtues. All of these virtues derive from the eight possible combinations of truth, love, and courage as follows:

Truth = *Honesty*
Love = *Compassion*
Courage = *Valor*
Truth + Love = *Justice*
Truth + Courage = *Honor*
Love + Courage = *Sacrifice*
Truth + Love + Courage = *Spirituality*
The absence of Truth, Love, and Courage is Pride, the opposite of which is *Humility*.

I found this system of virtues absolutely brilliant, especially coming from a game. Years later when I finally met Richard Garriott, designer of the Ultima series, at the Electronics Entertainment Expo (E3), I asked him how he came up with this system and how he ended up choosing these virtues. He told me it started with brainstorming a long list and noticing patterns in how the virtues related to each other.

As strange as it is that I got these insights from a game, I still think of living virtuously in much the same way today, where these eight virtues come about through the overlapping sets of truth, love, and courage. For the combination of all three virtues though, I feel that "integrity" is a better fit than "spirituality." Ultima V went on to explore the opposite of these, the vices which can be derived from falsehood, hatred, and cowardice. Unfortunately I feel the Ultima series really went downhill since then and completely lost its soul — I would have loved to have seen the virtue idea taken even farther.

I was thinking heavily in these terms when I started Dexterity Software in 1994. I did my best to hold true to living these virtues and integrated them into the company as much as I could. For example, in the roughly six years Dexterity has been sending out monthly royalty payments (many hundreds of payments total), not once has a single check ever gone out late, not even a day late. I don't know of any other game publisher who can claim the same, certainly none I've worked with. The commitment to do this was a matter of personal honor for me, and my personal concept of virtue was integrated into how I ran the business. Honor was always more important to me than profit . . . and still is.

The downside to attempting to live virtuously was that I got tossed around a lot by people who were clearly not living virtuously. Unfortunately the gaming industry is rife with such people, especially where large sums of money are concerned. I was well prepared to deal with other people who valued honor highly, but I was saddened to have the opportunity to do business with so few. Too many people placed money as a higher value than personal honor. So I was swimming against the tide. Even so, I still prefer this choice compared to the alternative.

I also began having a lot of internal conflicts while attempting to live virtuously. I don't blame the virtues for this though but rather my limited capacity for living in the fullest accordance with them. I was living my day-to-day life fairly virtuously, but what about the big picture? What about the very notion of running a game company for the purpose of entertaining people? Was that virtuous enough? I started pressing myself to do more, to push towards a higher ideal. I volunteered to serve as an officer in the Association of Shareware

Professionals for two years (zero pay). I wrote a lot of articles for free. I gave away a lot of advice and coached a lot of people for free. I spoke at conferences for free. I pushed myself to sacrifice more for the benefit of others. I bypassed some opportunities to make more money and instead pursued opportunities to provide more service.

I could sense this was an improvement for me, but still it didn't seem enough. I still didn't feel like I was close to optimal in terms of my ability to live virtuously. At first I figured this was just the nature of life, that this was to be a lifelong struggle. But I soon began feeling unsettled, perceiving that something wasn't quite right. For years I couldn't figure out what it was, so by default I stuck with what I knew. I had run into the same roadblock Aristotle may have hit, the one that prevented him from getting to the point of answering the question, "What is the best possible life?" I knew it was somewhere different than where I was, but I didn't know where to look.

What Is the Best Possible Life?

Eventually I came upon another way of approaching this problem of how to live. I asked myself, *Why is this such a difficult question anyway? What's so hard about it?* That started me along a new line of thinking which soon led me to this question: *What would have to change in order for this question to be easier to answer?*

Bingo.

It suddenly became clear why this question was so tough to answer. In order to answer it accurately, I'd have to know everything. I'd have to be God.

Let's face it. Our human intelligence is limited. Our technology is proof of that. My PC is better at arithmetic than I am. That tiny CPU can do a wide variety of tasks that my much larger brain cannot. My hard drive contains more data than I could memorize in a lifetime. Of course my brain has the CPU beat in many areas, but the point is that there are clearly intellectual limits to what our squishware can do.

I asked myself a lot of interesting questions to try to gain a new perspective on this. Can the mind comprehend its own limits? What if a superintelligent alien species came to earth — what would they see as the limits of human intelligence, and where would they perceive our boundaries? What can my brain clearly *not* do?

What if I were more intelligent than I am now? How might I live differently? What parts of my life would a more intelligent being consider foolish, unnecessary, or harmful? If a more intelligent being were to attempt to optimize my life, being able to clearly perceive my intellectual limits, what would it change? How would I optimize the life of a gorilla or a mouse if I could communicate with it? What do I perceive as their intellectual limits? What would the best possible life be for various other species?

And many, many more questions of this nature.

What eventually happened was that my context shifted. For the first time I felt I was actually running up against the limits of my own intelligence. I could begin to perceive where the walls were. Some of these limits were obvious, like the limits on my number crunching ability, memory, and speed. But I began to test other limits too. How many distinct concepts can I hold in my head at once? How accurately can I perceive time or temperature or weight without a measuring device?

How many problem-solving techniques do I really know, and
what are their strengths and weaknesses?

I started studying the brain in a little more detail and com-
paring my perceived mental limits to what was known about
the physical structure of the brain. The most current research
in this area is absolutely fascinating. By drugging the brain,
you can rob someone of consciousness. By electrically stimu-
lating a cluster of neurons, you can induce an experience the
subject would describe as spiritual (pushbutton spirituality?).
You can surgically remove a person's ability to play the piano.

As I developed a greater understanding of human intelligence, I realized that the biggest problem with the question
of how to live is that it requires a higher intelligence than we
now possess in order to answer it. In order to know what the
best possible life is, which is mathematically an optimization
problem, you have to know what all the possible lives are. And
that requires an amount of data which is currently impossible
for us to manage.

Imagine that there are only a million different variations on
how you could live your life. In order to choose the best one,
you have to look at all one million, apply some kind of criteria
to evaluate them, and then pick the one with the highest score.
There are three big problems with this. The first problem is that
there are too many options to reasonably consider. The second
problem is that you'd have to be able to accurately predict the
future to know how each life would turn out. And the third
problem is that you'd have to come up with the evaluation
criteria. The first two are clearly impossible right now, but
what about the third?

The third problem is basically what Aristotle attempted

to tackle — the evaluation criteria. Living virtuously is one possible answer, but it's still a bit fuzzy.

So we've got some serious problems here. First, we have a search space of possible solutions that's too big to fully explore. It's so big we can't even really comprehend the whole thing. And secondly, we need to figure out the evaluation criteria to intelligently compare one option to another, criteria that don't depend too heavily on the unknowable future.

Searching . . .

Let's tackle the first problem — that of the gigantic search space. First of all, finding a provably optimal solution is impossible. So the truest answer to the best way to live is that it's unknowable. We aren't smart enough to figure it out yet. That's not very satisfying, but it actually helps us a little. Now we're left with this question: How can we get close to the optimal solution?

Fortunately mathematics has an answer to this question: heuristics. A heuristic is a rule for exploring a search space that can help you get close to an optimal solution when you cannot explore the entire search space. An example heuristic would be hill-climbing. Imagine that you have a big 3D map to explore and you want to find the highest point. With hill-climbing, you'd start at a random point on the map and just make sure that every step you take is uphill. When you can't go uphill anymore, you've hit a peak — a local maximum. Without exploring more of the map, you can't be too sure your last hill was the highest one on the map, so you may continue to explore by starting at different points on the map and using the same hill-climbing heuristic. Unless you explore

the entire map, you can never be certain that you've found
the global maximum, but the more you explore, the more
confidence you gain.

So what does this mean for human living? It suggests a
hill-climbing approach to life. You try one way of living for a
while, and then you keep trying to improve upon it by taking
it "uphill." You tweak some of the parameters to make it better.
For example, you might try to lose weight, make more money,
or improve your relationships — any or all of these might be
considered a step uphill. And you just keep going uphill until
you can't go any higher.

Of course the problem with this approach is due to the
nature of heuristics — you may get stuck in a local maximum
that is far below the possible global maximum. The peak you're
striving to reach may only be a molehill in the grand scheme
of things. Another problem is that it could take you more than
a lifetime just to climb a single hill. You might die before you
get very far with this approach.

Ah, but as human beings we have a powerful asset on our
side that makes this problem a bit more manageable — imagination. We don't have to test these permutations physically.
We can test them in our minds. But this is only going to work
well if our mental map of reality is a close approximation of
real reality. In other words our simulation had better be very
close to the real thing, or our approximations will be way off,
and our results will be worthless. In order to have a chance at
succeeding at this, we have to accept reality as it truly is — all
of it, no matter what we must face about ourselves and how
unwilling we are to face it. Otherwise our simulation will be
full of glitches. Things that seem to work in our imaginations
won't work in the real world.

The more accurate your mental model of reality, the greater your ability to intelligently assess possible ways of living. This means you must know yourself in all your nakedness, both the good, the bad, and the ugly. You must develop a deep understanding of your own nature as you truly are. You must bring your beliefs into alignment with your actions. You must be internally congruent, or your simulations will only spew out garbage that you won't be able to trust.

I am not certain that everyone has the capacity to do this very well. It requires a high degree of intelligence and concentration to imagine what it would be like to live an alternative life and to assess it objectively. But it's all we have to deal with. We can only do our best.

I think the optimal solution would be to consider various ways you might live your life, vividly imagine each one in your imagination, and assess its strengths and weaknesses. Once you've covered a certain number of these (and I don't have a good way to know how many is enough — the more, the better), then you pick one and start living that way. Meanwhile, you continue to remain open to imagining other possibilities, and if you ever perceive one that is better than your current manner of living, you switch to the new "higher" life.

How Do You Compare One Life to Another?

Now we have to consider the evaluation criteria. What is uphill? How do we compare one life to another?

Many people have attempted to provide an answer to this question. One of the most popular answers in self-help today is happiness. We're told to do what makes us most happy. Seek pleasure. Avoid pain. Almost everything I've read about personal development uses some variation of happiness as the ultimate goal of life.

But I think happiness is a cop-out answer. Happiness is just an emotion. And placing my entire life in the service of achieving and maintaining a particular emotional state is clearly suboptimal. For one, I'm very emotionally resilient, and it doesn't take much to make me happy and content. Happiness and well-being can be maintained largely with a very healthy diet and lots of exercise. I'm already good at managing my emotions and being happy, so I'm certain I can do better than this.

Even if we extend happiness into the realm of fulfillment or flourishing, it's still a cop-out. By giving such an answer to the question of how to live, all we're doing is tossing the question over to our emotional intelligence. We're saying that the answer to how to live is whatever our emotions say is the answer. The assumption is that if we feel fulfilled, we must be living optimally. I see no logical reason this answer would be correct, given what I know about how emotions work. Not good enough.

For these reasons I rejected any answers that suggested the optimal manner of living was to be found in some kind of emotional state or feeling. I can consciously choose to feel whatever I want just by changing my focus. There isn't any particular course of action that will induce a feeling in me I can't achieve just by directing my imagination. I can self-emote.

And then we have a whole host of other self-help gurus who seem to define the goal of life in terms of being successful, becoming wealthy, having fulfilling relationships, etc. Well, as you probably suspect, that's just marketing fluff with no real substance behind it. Most of these books are aimed at trying to show you how to achieve optimal results within the pre-existing social context, but as we've already seen, even if you can manage to hit the supposed peak there, you'll still be living suboptimally. You'll only spend your whole life trying to climb a molehill and will leave most of your potential greatness untapped.

The way I chose to tackle this question was to look at my life in the context of the big picture of my clearest understanding of reality. This meant looking at the history of life to the degree we understand it, the possible future of life and where it might lead, and the present condition of life. I felt that a consideration of the best possible human life would have to be placed within the framework of all of life, past, present, and projected future. When I look at how life has evolved on earth, I see this force of evolution as something much greater than my own personal existence. I see that life has been continuing to upgrade its complexity, its intelligence, and its overall chances of survival. When I place myself within this context, I see that I have three basic options. I can work to cooperate with evolution, I can work against it, or I can ignore it. My human awareness gives me the ability to make this choice consciously.

As Close to Optimal As I Can Get

I decided that the best possible life would have to lie within the realm of cooperating with evolution rather than working against it. So for me this implies two things: 1) Working to evolve myself as an individual to the highest degree possible, and 2) Working to help life itself evolve to the highest degree possible. It turns out these goals are highly compatible, since there's a positive feedback loop between evolving yourself and evolving your environment. If you only work on yourself, your environment will ultimately hold you back. You'll be like Tarzan living among the apes. And if you only work to help others, that would also be suboptimal because you'll only be able to teach them what you know right now, but you'll never upgrade your knowledge and grow in your capacity to teach. So a balance of both is required.

For me this boils down to working on my own personal growth and helping others to grow. This became my means of assessing the best possible life I could hope to live.

So what does it mean to grow? To me it means to continually strive to upgrade my most powerful evolutionary assets, which I perceive as my intelligence, my consciousness, and my knowledge of reality. And in order to help others grow as well, I must consequently continue to upgrade my communication skills.

I see the main purpose of my life as serving the process of evolution. This is more important to me than anything else. Everything else in my life is secondary compared to this and must justify its fitness for this agenda. Who cares about getting a job and making money when you have the opportunity to consciously participate in the evolution of life itself? For me all other potential ways of living are nothing but pale shadows compared to this.

Let's tie this back in with the concept of heuristics now. This yields the following overall strategy:

Attempt to imagine the best possible life you can live with the evaluation criteria of serving the process of evolution itself.

Live it — experience it.

Whenever you become convinced that there is a better way for you to serve the process of evolution than what you're doing now, transition to it.

This is my answer to the question of how to live: to invest the bulk of my life in the pursuit of growth. To me this makes perfect sense. If we cannot fathom how to live optimally, then the best solution would be to develop a greater capacity to do so. If your computer is incapable of doing what you need it to do, then you should invest your time working to upgrade the computer.

I find this answer also combines well with Aristotle's concept of virtue. Intelligence suggests a direction, and virtue helps mold the path. I believe both are essential for living the best possible life. Of the two though, I think intelligence is the more powerful, since the virtues themselves were derived from our human intelligence. One way of thinking of the virtues is as intellectual shortcuts. If there is too much data to make a truly intelligent decision, you can fall back on the virtues and trust that they are at least not likely to be stupid choices. When in doubt, be honest, be honorable, be brave.

Squishware 2.0

If you suddenly found yourself living as an ape, you could accept the life of an ape and devote yourself to eating bananas all day and try to be a good ape, or you could attempt to become more than an ape and evolve into a human. Once you did that, all your ape goals and accomplishments would seem utterly meaningless compared to your new human capabilities. How silly will goals like building a business or becoming good at marketing appear to a more evolved species?

On the evolutionary ladder, we're just a bunch of apes right now. But if we keep growing, we will soon be much more. It's likely that computer technology will more closely merge with our own squishware to make us ever smarter and more capable. But even before that happens, we can continue learning more about our squishware and push it to its limits. Let's stop living on 3% of our brainpower and crank it closer to 100%.

There are many ways to consciously assist the process of evolution, and our ability to do this right now is of course limited (although more of these limits are collapsing each year). Over the course of a lifetime, I think one person living today who devotes his/her life to assisting the evolution of our species can have a dramatic effect. We still remember Aristotle for his contribution. What more could we accomplish if thousands of us living today devoted our lives to a similar purpose?

I have no way to prove this to you, but I seem to be discovering that the more I work to align my life with the process of evolution, the more my life flows almost effortlessly, as if I'm being magnetically pulled along. For the past year my life has been working extremely well, and I feel like I'm able to think more clearly than ever. This was a recent context switch for me, just within the past year, but I feel as if it's growing stronger each month. It's a feeling of clarity that this is just what I'm meant to do with my life. Self-discipline is still required, but I'm stronger and more able to apply it consistently. I think the reason is that I finally feel I am indeed living the best possible life I'm capable of, given what I know right now. When I try to imagine something better, it's only an increase in my capacity to do the same thing, not a change in the essence of what I'm doing. Getting to this point, however, was not remotely easy, and I'm certain that more change lies ahead. That is the nature of growth — old goals are constantly in the process of becoming obsolete.

Next, we'll explore how to translate this high-level notion of how to live into a personal purpose that is actually achievable. Then we'll cover how to break that purpose down into goals, projects, and actions and get moving on it.

Chapter 3

Discover Your Purpose

Do You Have a Pre-Encoded Purpose?

Many books I've read seem to assume that we're either genetically or divinely encoded with some sort of built-in purpose, and all we need to do is take the time to discover it through private introspection. You just sit down one day and write a mission statement and trust that what comes out of you will be the guiding force for the rest of your life. Perhaps every 6–12 months you update it.

Personally I think that's nonsense. I see no evidence that there's any pre-encoded purpose in any of us. You may have experienced strong social conditioning towards a particular purpose, such as if you're born a prince or princess, and certainly your DNA will control some aspects of your life, but that isn't sufficient evidence of any sort of divine will at work. I think in most cases you'll just end up with a wishy-washy mission statement that doesn't mean much.

If you begin with the assumption that you have a pre-encoded purpose and attempt to discover it merely by sitting down and writing a mission statement, I think you'll end up building a house of straw for yourself. You won't have a rational foundation for trusting your purpose. In most cases you'll feel like you're just guessing, and you might look back on your mission statement a week later and find that it's not so interesting as you thought it was when you wrote it. You'll always have doubts about what you've written.

When people try to sit down and write out a purpose or mission statement, they usually lack sufficient clarity to do so intelligently. How exactly are you supposed to define your purpose? Are you simply supposed to know it and squeeze it out of your brain like a sponge? What if you can imagine several different missions that might fit you, but you have no idea which is better? What if you can't think of anything at all that seems meaningful to you? What then?

Just because you may not have a pre-encoded purpose doesn't mean you don't have a purpose, though. It simply means that it will take more work to define your purpose. Your purpose isn't really something you discover. It would be more accurate to say that your purpose is something you co-create based on your relationship to reality. I wouldn't exactly call it a free choice though. There may be multiple choices for you, but all choices are not equally valid.

What is needed is an intelligent method for developing your purpose, a process that makes sense, such that when you arrive at your final answer, you have high trust that it's correct.

Why Does Purpose Matter?

Why does it matter whether or not your life actually has a purpose?

Let's take a few steps back and creep up on this question. . . .

If you complete a task, and there's no overall important context for that task, then the task doesn't really matter. So you watch a TV show. It doesn't make a difference — there's no larger context for it. But if you complete a task that's part of a larger project, now it suddenly matters, at least within the context of the project. If you create a web page, and it's part of a new web site you're building, that task matters. It takes you closer to the realization of the completed project.

Now when does a project matter? Projects matter only within the context of a larger goal. If your goal is to increase your income, and you complete a project that is likely to facilitate it, the project matters. It brings you a step closer to the realization of your goal. But if you complete a project like digging a trench through your backyard, and there's no real goal you're trying to accomplish, then the project is pointless. There's no meaning behind it.

If a project isn't part of some larger goal, then that project has no context and is therefore irrelevant. You don't need a complicated goal to give meaning to a project. It could be something simple like increasing your happiness or even just entertaining you for a while. But human behavior is purposeful, and we humans don't tend to undertake projects if there is no good reason for doing so. People don't often work hard at digging holes and refilling them for no reason.

What's the difference between projects and goals? Goals are outcomes, objectives. They're states of being — a state where you'd like to be at some point. Projects are encapsulations of the actions you feel you can take to help you achieve a goal. Owning your own home is a goal. Writing a screenplay is a project.

So to reverse the order, you start by setting some goals, create projects to achieve those goals, and perform tasks to complete those projects and thereby achieve your goals.

But now what's the context for your goals? Why do they matter? If a task needs the context of a project and a project needs the context of a goal, don't goals need a context as well in order for them to matter?

Say you set a goal to increase your income by 50%. Why is that relevant? Is it pointless? What is the context within which such a goal actually matters? Why is that goal any better or worse than filling your backyard with holes?

Goals do need a context as well; otherwise, they're irrelevant too. A goal without a meaningful larger context is pointless.

One context that makes goals matter is human need, branching from the basic root need of survival. Goals that enhance your survival can be said to be important. Another human need is connecting with others; it's been found that this need is actually hardwired into us from birth.

But if all our goals occur only within the context of physical and emotional needs, then all we really get out of life is survival and mediocrity. Making more money seems to help satisfy our need for security. Getting married and having kids helps with our need for socialization and connection. And then there are compound behaviors like learning new skills to advance in our careers so we can become better and better at filling these basic needs.

But there's another possible context for our goals that goes beyond need. And that is the context of purpose. If your life has a purpose other than merely satisfying your own physical and emotional needs, now you have the ability to access a whole new arena of goal-setting. You can set goals that go way beyond the context of need.

Some people may argue that purpose is a human need as well, possibly a spiritual need. I suppose that's a valid way of looking at it, except that it doesn't appear to be as much of a *need* as physical and emotional survival — it's a lot quieter and easier to tune out. But for now I'll treat purpose as something above and beyond basic physical and emotional needs.

If you only work within the context of need, then you automatically lack the ability to set and achieve certain types of goals. There are some goals you'll just never be able to achieve. You don't have a context for them, so you'll never set them in the first place. Even though they might be grand and interesting goals, you won't even consider them. People who achieve those kinds of goals that lie outside your context might include Jesus, Mother Teresa, Gandhi, and Martin Luther King, Jr. They worked within a context beyond personal need. If your only context for goals is need, then you can never hope to get close to anything they did. Your whole life will only be about survival — that's as far as you'll go. All you can ever hope for is mediocrity; greatness lies beyond your reach.

The second problem with having need as your only context for goals is that you'll have a hard time pushing yourself beyond the point where you feel your needs are already satisfied. For some of you reading this, you've probably already done pretty well at setting and achieving goals within the context of your personal needs. I've been at this point in my life for many years. All my basic needs are met, and I expect I'll be able to maintain that situation for the rest of my life without too much trouble. So there's no real motivation in pushing myself to set more goals within the context of need. All that context can do is keep me maintaining the status quo, at best edging it up gradually. It can help me achieve more of the same and sometimes even an improved version of the same, but it can't help drive me to achieve goals outside the context of need. And there are a lot of hugely interesting goals and experiences that don't fall within the realm of need.

Some people get a lot more mileage out of the need context than others. For example, if you're starting from a point of poverty, the context of need alone can push you to become extremely wealthy. Similarly, a bout with cancer can enable you to push yourself to a far greater state of health in the long run. But for most people, at some point that context of need runs dry. You can tell if this has happened to you if, when you think about big goals, they just don't seem to matter; they appear to be more trouble than they're worth. You have an underlying feeling that says, "Eh . . . why bother?" I suppose this helps explain why 90% of the people working today can expect to earn within +/- 10% of their current income for the rest of their lives.

When you reach this point of stuckness, it's time to move beyond the context of need. Think of your need context as being a project you've completed. There's no point in continuing to perform tasks within the scope of a project that's already done. If you've already made dinner and eaten it, you can stop stirring the sauce. The meal is done.

Similarly, if you're now living in a situation where your needs are adequately met, and you don't seem to be getting any more mileage out of need-based goals, then you need a new context for goal setting. Otherwise, you'll be stuck with some lame and impotent goals. You're probably in this situation now if you set a goal to double your income, and despite feeling like you should want to achieve it, you get nowhere with it. And you know it's because you didn't really put much effort into it. Again, it seems more trouble than it's worth. You're not impotent though — your context for setting this goal is impotent. It doesn't tap into your passion and talents in a way that sustains your momentum.

The next context beyond need is purpose. Purpose doesn't conflict with need. It's just a new context for goal setting. It can continue to coexist with need-based goals. Just as you can have multiple projects and multiple goals in your life, you can also have multiple goal contexts.

The cool thing about purpose is that it's a much more expansive and interesting context than need. Need is pretty limited, as it's focused around survival. But purpose is a much broader context that frees you from the limits of working on survival goals. Ideally, your purpose will be found within the overlap between your passion and your talents.

I also find that the context of purpose works better than the context of need in several ways. First, it aligns better with your inner fire . . . your passion. You can only get semi-passionate about meeting your needs, but when your passion is aligned with your purpose, you'll have far more energy and get far more done. For example, if you're trying to find a mate out of the context of need, like you don't want to be alone the rest of your life, that's very weak motivation. You can easily fail to achieve such a goal when it's only motivated by need — there's little passion behind it . . . more of a sense of desperation. And your drive will be inconsistent — some days you'll feel it strongly, while other days it will be weaker, and you'll feel OK being alone. But when you come from the context of purpose, you're feeling great about who you are as a human being, thinking about how much you have to offer a potential mate, and radiating that feeling to others you meet. And that passion will make it far easier to attract someone compatible into your life. Desperation turns people away, but passion attracts. Think about it — how attracted would you be to a potential mate who is living his/her purpose vs. someone whose whole life is just about survival? And if you attract someone from your need-based context, that person will most likely be in that same context, so your whole relationship will exist within the context of need — I need you; you need me. But contrast this with a relationship which forms within the context of purpose for both people; now the relationship itself can be much broader because it transcends need. The relationship itself forms out of the basis of achieving a greater purpose. These aren't always romantic relationships either — you can see outcomes like the relationship between Jesus and his Apostles, coming together from a context of purpose rather than need.

The second way that purpose works better than need is that purpose is a more stable context. Need is a great motivator when you're starving, but it's a lousy motivator when your belly is full. The more you achieve your goals within the context of need, the more that need is satisfied, and the weaker it becomes as a context for setting new goals. Purpose, however, is ongoing and doesn't drop off in intensity as you achieve success. It maintains its power at more constant levels — in fact, if anything it grows stronger the more you work within it.

Thirdly, self-discipline becomes easier. When your passion and talents are aligned with your goals (which is what happens within the context of purpose), everything down the line gets easier. Most of the projects and tasks which derive from your purpose-driven goals will fall within your talents, unlike need-based goals, which can lead to projects and actions that are very difficult and stressful. For example, if your purpose involves composing beautiful music, and you have a strong innate talent in this area, then your projects and tasks will likely involve spending a lot of time composing music. You don't have to force yourself into action, since you're already good at this kind of work, and you enjoy it immensely too. But you don't always have this luxury of aligning passion and talents when you work only within the context of need. That's where you may have to do things that you dislike and which you aren't very good at, like forcing the musician inside you to do accounting work. Instead of feeling energized all day long, you'll feel drained and demotivated if you work too far outside your passion-talent bubble for too long.

Fourthly, you'll find that when you work within the context of purpose, you'll also be able to use this context to more powerfully satisfy some of your needs automatically. Think back to the lower level of projects. Sometimes if you complete a particular project, it automatically takes care of another project in the process — i.e. killing two birds with one stone. You can do the same thing when working on goals from different contexts. And when this happens, it's wonderful because you can achieve need-based goals while still enjoying the benefits of working within the context of purpose. An example here would be if you decide to pursue your passion as a musician, and you become very financially successful at it. So now you're able to use your talents and passion to handle your physical needs without having to succumb to doing things you dislike or which you aren't very good at. You're able to satisfy your needs while staying within your passion-talent bubble.

This makes it pretty clear that knowing your purpose is crucial. If you don't have a purpose in life, then you're stuck working only within the context of need. It means your life is only about physical and emotional survival. Certain goals are forever beyond your ability to achieve. And your ongoing motivation for setting and achieving goals will become weaker the more successful you are at achieving them. The further you get, the weaker your motivation for continued goal-setting. The best you can hope for within this context is pretty darn limited. You're basically doomed to live out a complicated version of life as a lower mammal.

However, when you know your purpose, now you have a whole new context for goal setting . . . not only new but also a lot more powerful. Imagine spending your whole life up to this point working on a project that isn't very interesting to you and which you're not very good at. And then suddenly you're given a second project which fascinates you and which is a perfect fit for your skills and talents. And on top of that, if you focus on this new second project, it will likely take care of the first project automatically, so you never have to work on the first project directly again. Now which project would you choose to work on?

You don't have to master the survival context to begin working in the purpose context. By it's very nature, you can't really ever master survival — the better you get at meeting your needs, the weaker this context becomes. And you needn't abandon the survival context either. Keep setting need-based goals. But add that second, more powerful context of purpose right alongside it. Now you have a new dimension to start setting goals that have nothing to do with your survival needs.

What can you do within the context of purpose that you can't do within the context of need? You can create an album of your own beautiful music with no concern over making money from it . . . just the desire to share it with the world. And you can have it matter deeply to you and not feel irrelevant and pointless. What are some goals you can set within the context of purpose which lie outside the context of need?

When you expand your goal-setting into the context of purpose, you expand your life. Right now I'd say I'm spending about 80% of my work time on goals within my purpose context and about 20% in the need context. A year ago it was about 80–20 the opposite way. This has made a huge positive difference for me, with the best part being that I've been experiencing life in ways I'd never have been able to access from the context of need alone. Often it's possible to take a need-based goal and transform it into a purpose-based goal. So you gain access to all the motivational benefits of the purpose context while still taking care of the basic need.

If you don't yet know your purpose, it's worthwhile to take the time to discover it, so you can get past the dull need context and start working on some far more interesting purpose-driven goals congruent with your deepest passion and your greatest talents.

Chapter 4

How to Intelligently Define Your Purpose

How do you discover your real purpose in life? I'm not talking about your job, your daily responsibilities, or even your long-term goals. I mean the real reason why you're here at all — the very reason you exist.

I'm going to suggest two different methods for defining your purpose. Ideally you should use both of them, since each will help you understand different aspects of your purpose. This is going to be a lot of work, but the end result will be worth it because you'll reach a point of tremendous clarity. In the end it will be far easier to make decisions and take action, and you'll find that your life just seems to work once you know your purpose.

Method 1: Emotional Intelligence

The first method is to consult your emotional intelligence. Passion and purpose go hand in hand. When you discover your purpose, you will normally find it's something you're tremendously passionate about. Emotionally you will feel that it is correct.

Perhaps you're a rather nihilistic person who doesn't believe you have a purpose and that life has no meaning. Doesn't matter. Not believing that you have a purpose won't prevent you from discovering it, just as a lack of belief in gravity won't prevent you from tripping. All that a lack of belief will do is make it take longer. Most likely though if you don't believe you have a purpose, then you probably won't believe what I'm saying anyway, but even so, what's the risk of investing an hour just in case?

Here's a story about Bruce Lee which sets the stage for this little exercise. A master martial artist asked Bruce to teach him everything Bruce knew about martial arts. Bruce held up two cups, both filled with liquid. "The first cup," said Bruce, "represents all of your knowledge about martial arts. The second cup represents all of my knowledge about martial arts. If you want to fill your cup with my knowledge, you must first empty your cup of your knowledge."

If you want to discover your true purpose in life, you must first empty your mind of all the false purposes you've been taught (including the idea that you may have no purpose at all).

So how to discover your purpose in life? While there are many ways to do this, some of them fairly involved, here is one of the simplest that anyone can do. The more open you are to this process, and the more you expect it to work, the faster it will work for you. But not being open to it or having doubts about it or thinking it's an entirely idiotic and meaningless waste of time won't prevent it from working as long as you stick with it — again, it will just take longer to converge.

Here's what to do:

Take out a blank sheet of paper or open up a word processor where you can type (I prefer the latter because it's faster).

Write at the top, "What is my true purpose in life?"

Write an answer (any answer) that pops into your head. It doesn't have to be a complete sentence. A short phrase is fine.

Repeat step 3 until you write the answer that makes you cry. This is your purpose.

That's it. It doesn't matter if you're a counselor or an engineer or a bodybuilder. To some people this exercise will make perfect sense. To others it will seem utterly stupid. Usually it takes 15–20 minutes to clear your head of all the clutter and the social conditioning about what you think your purpose in life is. The false answers will come from your mind and your memories. But when the true answer finally arrives, it will feel like it's coming to you from a different source entirely.

For those who are very entrenched in low-awareness living, it will take a lot longer to get all the false answers out, possibly more than an hour. But if you persist, after 100 or 200 or maybe even 500 answers, you'll be struck by the answer that causes you to surge with emotion, the answer that breaks you. If you've never done this, it may very well sound silly to you. So let it seem silly, and do it anyway.

As you go through this process, some of your answers will be very similar. You may even re-list previous answers. Then you might head off on a new tangent and generate 10–20 more answers along some other theme. And that's fine. You can list whatever answer pops into your head as long as you just keep writing.

At some point during the process (typically after about 50–100 answers), you may want to quit and just can't see it converging. You may feel the urge to get up and make an excuse to do something else. That's normal. Push past this resistance, and just keep writing. The feeling of resistance will eventually pass.

You may also discover a few answers that seem to give you a mini-surge of emotion, but they don't quite make you cry — they're just a bit off. Highlight those answers as you go along, so you can come back to them to generate new permutations. Each reflects a piece of your purpose, but individually they aren't complete. When you start getting these kinds of answers, it just means you're getting warm. Keep going.

It's important to do this alone and with no interruptions. If you're a nihilist, then feel free to start with the answer, "I don't have a purpose," or "Life is meaningless," and take it from there. If you keep at it, you'll still eventually converge.

When you find your own unique answer to the question of why you're here, you will feel it resonate with you deeply. The words will seem to have a special energy to you, and you will feel that energy whenever you read them.

Discovering your purpose is the easy part. The hard part is keeping it with you on a daily basis and working on yourself to the point where you become that purpose.

If you're inclined to ask why this little process works, just put that question aside until after you've successfully completed it. Once you've done that, you'll probably have your own answer to why it works. Most likely if you ask 10 different people why this works (people who've successfully completed it), you'll get

10 different answers, all filtered through their individual belief systems, and each will contain its own reflection of truth.

Obviously, this process won't work if you quit before convergence. I'd guesstimate that 80–90% of people should achieve convergence in less than an hour. If you're really entrenched in your beliefs and resistant to the process, maybe it will take you 5 sessions and 3 hours, but I suspect that such people will simply quit early (like within the first 15 minutes) or won't even attempt it at all. But if you're drawn to read this (and haven't been inclined to ban it from your life yet), then it's doubtful you fall into this group.

The answer you get from this process depends heavily on your ability to generate good input. Essentially what you are doing is exploring the search space of possible purposes, and you're using the heuristic of your emotional reaction to gauge how close you are. But one thing I failed to mention in the original explanation of this process is that it requires you're clear about your overall context for life first. If you don't have that level of clarity yet, then you'll have a hard time making this approach work successfully — you'll be approaching the problem from the wrong context, so the potential answers you generate will all be in the wrong neighborhood. Garbage in, garbage out.

To use an analogy, imagine you're looking at a map of the United States, trying to locate Las Vegas. If you have a good map, it shouldn't take you long at all. Your eyes might shoot towards the left (west) side of the map, slide right (east) from California to Nevada, and you'll soon spot Las Vegas in Southern Nevada. But what if you try this same exercise using a map of the U.S. from 1870. Now that's a problem because Las Vegas didn't officially become a city until 1911, so you won't find it on a map from 1870. You won't be able to locate the city until you realize you're looking at an inaccurate map and get yourself a more recent map. Similarly, if your context is an inaccurate fit for reality, corrupted by too many false beliefs and incorrect assumptions, then you're unlikely to be able to define a meaningful purpose for your life no matter what method you use — it's simply not to be found anywhere on your map. Most likely you'll settle for something that's close to your purpose, but not quite right. You may target Reno instead of Las Vegas (Reno became a city in 1868, so it might be seen on your 1870 map).

When I did this exercise, it took me about 25 minutes, and I reached my final answer at step 106. Partial pieces of the answer (mini-surges) appeared at steps 17, 39, and 53, and then the bulk of it fell into place and was refined through steps 100–106. I felt the feeling of resistance (wanting to get up and do something else, expecting the process to fail, feeling very impatient and even irritated) around steps 55–60. At step 80 I took a 2-minute break to close my eyes, relax, clear my mind, and to focus on the intention for the answer to come to me — this was helpful as the answers I received after this break began to have greater clarity.

Here was my final answer: *to live consciously and coura- geously, to resonate with love and compassion, to awaken the great spirits within others, and to leave this world in peace.*

You may notice certain patterns in this purpose statement that link up with my overall concept of reality:

to live consciously = awareness, required for conscious personal growth

and courageously = courage, a virtue required to pursue conscious growth

to resonate with love = unconditional love, which isn't an emotion but rather a sense of connectedness with everything that exists, implying that working on my own growth and helping others to grow are compatible

and compassion = another virtue, one which helps temper courage

to awaken the great spirits within others = to help others lock in at a higher level of consciousness/awareness, which will give them the means to pursue personal growth consciously

and to leave this world in peace = a double meaning here: 1) world in peace = to do no harm, to work to improve life instead of destroy it, to leave a legacy; 2) leave . . . in peace = no regrets, knowing I did my best and could have expected no more of myself, refusing to die with my music still in me, inner peace

Method 2: Rational Intelligence

The second method is to use your reason and logic to work down from your context. The clearer and more accurate your context is, the easier this will be.

To identify your purpose, you basically project your entire context of reality onto yourself. Given your current understanding of reality, where do you fit in? If you buy into the social context that most people seem to use, this will be virtually impossible for the reasons stated in yesterday's post. Social contexts don't provide sufficient clarity. At best you may end up with a wishy-washy purpose statement that addresses the basics like making money, having a family, having friends, and being nice, but there won't be any real substance to it. If you gave it to someone else to read it, they wouldn't come away knowing you any better.

Fuzzy context, fuzzy projection, fuzzy purpose.

Clear context, clear projection, clear purpose.

Since my context of reality is based on seeing life as a process of ongoing evolution (and I use the term evolution merely in the sense of growth and change, not in the strictly biological sense via natural selection), then when I project this context onto myself, the result is very simple — I'm a participant in the process of growth and change.

This is such a simple approach that it's easy to miss. All you're really doing is looking at your overall context of life and projecting those same qualities onto yourself. This projection becomes your purpose, your role in reality.

Imagine a hologram. When you cut off a piece of a hologram, the entire original image is still contained within the smaller piece. Reality is the big hologram, and you're a piece of it. You inherit all the properties of reality. Your beliefs about reality become your beliefs about yourself. If your beliefs are accurate, you'll end up with a sensible, achievable purpose.

This method will also help you identify problems in your context because you'll notice that something is wrong when you project a false belief onto yourself.

Suppose your context of reality is whatever the Catholic Church teaches. Then when you project this context on yourself, you get that your purpose is to serve God, obey the Church in religious matters, and to strive to be like Jesus.

If you have a null context of reality (nihilism), you get a null purpose. When you project nothing onto X, you get nothing.

If you don't like the purpose you end up with when applying this method, then what you're really saying is that you don't like the context you're using. This is a conflict you'll need to resolve. You must either accept the context and the purpose that accompanies it, or you must change the context.

Blending the Two Methods

I think it's helpful to use both methods for defining your purpose to see where they lead you. If your context is sound, you should get congruent answers from both approaches. Your emotional and rational intelligences will each phrase your purpose differently, but you should see that it's essentially the same. But most of the time that won't be the case, and the answers will be different, which means your context is incongruent. You rationally think about reality in one way but you feel it in another way. Perhaps you hold religious beliefs but only follow them sporadically — they aren't integrated across your entire life. You may feel in your heart that your beliefs are true, but you don't think them in your head. In this case you have to identify the disparity, figure out where it comes from, and work it through until you can get both sides to agree or you can get clear on which one is correct. Use your consciousness to listen to the emotional side and the rational side, and be like a negotiator between them.

For example, if emotionally you feel that your purpose is to be some kind of artist or musician, but rationally you work out that you should be serving people in need, then you have to work through this disconnect by taking a look at what your context says about it. Remember that your context is your collection of beliefs about reality. When you experience a conflict like this, it will typically lead you to a hole in your context, a fuzzy area that you haven't yet clarified. In this case you might see that you have mixed feelings as to the overall value of art and music. You partly see them as serving people, and you partly see them as a relative waste of time compared to other pursuits. You'll have to decide which is the most accurate, empowering viewpoint. You have to fill the hole in your context. Yesterday's post explains how to do that.

This can be a lengthy process if you have a very fuzzy concept of reality or if you're very conflicted internally. For many people this will require rooting out incongruencies and consciously filling contextual holes, and it will take a long time before enough of those are eliminated to wield sufficient clarity to define a clear purpose.

At this point your purpose is likely to be very abstract and high-level, so next we'll explore how to break it down into goals, projects, and actions.

Chapter 5

From Purpose to Action

Once you've identified your overall purpose/mission, the next step is to turn that purpose into achievable goals, projects, and actions that would be congruent with that purpose.

Living Congruently

Do you tend to compartmentalize all the different areas of your life? Career goes there, relationship goes here, spirituality fits there, and health . . . well, that's neither here nor there.

Or maybe your compartmentalizing is temporal instead of spatial in your thinking. During the workday you do what you must, this evening you'll do what you love and have some fun, and on Sunday you'll think about what it means.

Or perhaps you experience a feeling of compartmentalizing thought vs. action: "I'm spending X% of my time thinking and Y% of my time acting."

When you view your life as a series of different compartments, each with different rules, then life gets pretty complicated. Trying to achieve balance is very difficult because you constantly feel the need to task switch. My relationship needs attention. Oh no, I've been neglecting my health. I need to work harder. I've got to stop thinking so much and take more action.

The different "bins" of your life are all fighting for your time. And the longer you neglect one of those bins, the louder it gets and the harder it will fight for attention. Put off your health for too long, and you'll crash with an illness. Put off your relationship for too long, and a breakup may be the result. Put off your work, and your career and income will suffer.

This is a paradigm that many people share. Keep all your balls in the air. Keep all those plates spinning. Don't let your spiritual beliefs interfere with your work.

But I think it's a broken paradigm. Let's consider a different way of thinking. . . .

What if your life had only one bin, one ball to juggle, one plate to spin. Just one. No need to deal with 10 different areas of your life and keep them all balanced. Just one.

How is this possible? It's possible if all of those different areas of your life are congruent, if they all follow the same rules. Then thought and action are one, both pointing in the same direction. They're on the same path. Your work is congruent with your most deeply held spiritual beliefs — you don't have to take your spirituality offline when you go to work. Improving your health improves your relationship. Increasing your income increases your service.

This means moving from a paradigm of the different parts of your life being in conflict to a new paradigm where they all cooperate. Instead of seeing each part of your life as independent, you begin to see them as interdependent. And isn't this a more accurate model anyway? Can you truly isolate each part of your life as something separate? Can you abuse your health and think it won't affect your career or your relationships? Do you think your feelings about your relationship won't affect your financial situation? Can you ignore your spiritual beliefs when making business decisions and expect no negative consequences?

It seems obvious that all the different parts of your life are deeply interconnected. But a common way to treat problems is to try to isolate them. If there's a problem with your health, you need to diet and exercise. If there's a problem in your career, it's time to work harder. But this isolation protocol doesn't work well because there's too much overlap between all the different parts of your life, no matter how much you try to isolate the problem areas and go to work on them.

It's often the case that the obvious cause of the problem isn't the true source. If you feel lonely because you haven't been able to find the right relationship, and you keep trying harder and harder to find a relationship, you may get nowhere. The problem may be that you work at a career you aren't passionate about, and you project this lack of passion to everyone you meet. And still a deeper issue may be that your spiritual beliefs tell you that service to others is very important, but you don't feel you're doing that. Then you change careers to do what you love, and it aligns with your spiritual beliefs because now you feel you're contributing and serving. Then out of nowhere, you meet your future spouse, who is attracted to your passion about your work and the contribution you're making. And the encouragement you experience from this relationship in turn helps you advance your career, increase your income, and free up more time to spend with your new spouse. Your stress goes down, and your health improves too. Your inner spiritual conflict was the real source of your inability to find the right relationship. Everything is deeply interconnected.

Although it seems that each part of your life follows different rules, they all follow the same rules. You may have different values for each part of your life, but the rules that govern those areas don't change.

An example of an unchanging rule is kindness. The concept of kindness should resonate with your spiritual beliefs. You can be kind to your body, and your health will improve. You can be kind to your co-workers, and your relationships with them will improve. You can be kind to your spouse, and your marriage will grow stronger. You can be kind to a stranger, and your self-esteem will increase. It doesn't matter to which area of your life you apply the principle of kindness. Its application is universal.

Another universal rule is being proactive, assuming personal responsibility for results and taking positive action. It doesn't matter where you apply this rule: health, relationships, emotions, spiritual beliefs, career, business, money, etc. Being responsible works no matter where you apply it.

Cheating is another universal principle. No matter where you apply it, the long-term results are negative. Cheat your health, and pay the price of sickness. Cheat in your relationship, and the cost is a loss of intimacy. Cheat in your education, and your income suffers.

But more powerful than these intra-area effects, there's the rippling effect due to the interrelatedness of all areas. So if you apply a universal principle in one area, either positively or negatively, it ripples into all other areas. If you cheat your health, then in the long run this will hurt your career, your relationships, your finances, your emotional state, and your sense of spiritual connectedness. You can't cheat in one area of your life without suffering the consequences in ALL areas.

Similarly, be kind to your body, and your increased positive energy will positively affect your relationships, your work, your finances, your emotions, etc. Be proactive about building a career you enjoy, and your passion will spread to every other area.

If you violate a universal principle, it negatively impacts all areas of your life. If you follow a universal principle, it positively impacts all areas of your life. Universal principles don't compartmentalize.

So the key then is figuring out these universal principles and aligning your thoughts and actions with them. This is how you achieve congruence between all the different parts of your life.

So what are the universal principles? Stephen Covey claims that the *7 Habits of Highly Effective People* are based on universal principles. I tend to agree, and that's a good place to start. But I think all of these principles can be reduced to just one: to love. Not the passive squishy emotional feeling of love, but "to love" — the action verb. To love your body translates into proper diet and exercise. To love your mind equates with learning. To love others is service. To love your work is to do it passionately and enthusiastically. To love your feelings means to respect and honor the messages they send you. This verb translates into different specific actions for each area, but the underlying principle is the same. Depending on the situation, "to love" may mean to listen, to serve, to work, to relax, to touch, and so on.

When you start injecting universal principles into every area of your life, alignment will gradually occur. The parts of your life will be transformed such that all these different pieces assemble themselves into one congruent whole. You won't feel like these different parts of your life are in competition for your time and attention. Instead you'll feel a sense of internal cooperation. You will have a sense that exercising your body is the best thing for your health and your relationship and your career and your spirituality.

Within each area you'll either adapt your current circumstances to align with universal principles, or you'll let go of all the misaligned pieces and start fresh. So your career may shift slightly as you adapt, or you may switch to a whole new career. Your old relationships may transform, or they may end while you seek out new ones. It just depends on how well the external parts of your life are able to align with who you are.

Alignment comes down to working on these four questions until they all produce the same answer:

> What do you *want* to do? (desire)
> What *can* you do? (ability)
> What *should* you do? (purpose)
> What *must* you do? (need)

When these four areas are aligned, motivation occurs automatically. Thought and action are automatically balanced because you are living your purpose consciously. You won't feel like you should be thinking when you're acting or acting when you're thinking. The line between thought and action will disappear. Being and doing will become the same thing.

When you experience misalignment between these four areas/questions, the natural tendency is to slow down . . . sometimes to a crawl. You'll feel like you have all these ideas pulling you in different directions, but you aren't fully satisfying any of them. Your mind knows that continuing to work hard is likely to be futile and won't solve the real problem of incongruence. It knows it's time for you to stop, ask directions, and choose the path of alignment.

I went through this while running my games business. While I had many projects to grow the business, I knew deep down that I didn't want to run that business for another decade. I was containerizing everything: my health over here, my relationship there, my work here, and my spirituality there. Each part of my life felt like it had its own set of rules. Eventually I started questioning whether this was the best way to live. Are we supposed to live like a collection of parts or as an integrated whole? I wondered whether it would be possible to live in such a way where there was only one set of rules governing all areas, essentially meaning that I followed my deepest spiritual beliefs in all matters. This line of questioning led me to discover just how it might be possible for all these different parts of my life to become a single, integrated whole. This would mean that my business and my conscience and my interpersonal relationships were all one. There would be no sense of separation.

In order to go through this process, I had to transform certain parts of my life while totally shifting others. I tried to transform my career initially from within, but the disconnect was big enough that it required a more dramatic shift. Other parts of my life were able to adapt more flexibly. The main reason for my shift away from my games business was that it wasn't a strong enough outlet for service for me. I think that given enough time, the original business could have been shifted, but that wasn't the best route for me too take. It was faster and simpler to build a new business from scratch with the goal of congruence in mind than to try to refactor the existing business.

I must say that this push for congruence in all areas turned out beautifully. I don't feel that sense of separation between the different parts of my life anymore. My purpose says I'm here to serve and help people. My ability says I can do it through writing and speaking and running a web site. My needs say I must support myself doing it. And my passion says it's what I love doing most. I don't have to separate supporting myself with a job and then having fun on the weekends and thinking about spirituality at other times. Work = play = love.

When you live congruently, it's as if all the different parts of your life lock into new positions to form a new whole that's greater than all the individual pieces. Everything grows stronger: health, relationships, motivation, actions, results, etc.

I know that as a practical matter, it seems as though different rules often govern in different areas. Separating your spiritual beliefs from your work is very common. A lot of businesses seem to operate on the assumption that universal principles don't exist. I don't buy that at all. There are non-universal principles that apply just within their own domains (the rules of nutrition apply to your health but not to your work, for instance), but universal principles apply to all areas. I think that one's spiritual beliefs are the single most important factor in choosing a career or a company to work for. If you have a deeply held belief that you hold sacred, you cannot violate it in any area of your life without suffering the consequences in all areas. You must be true to your inner self at all times. That's the only way to be congruent and to live as a whole person instead of merely as a bag of competing parts.

When you live congruently, a quantum leap will occur in each of these four areas. Desire becomes passion. Purpose becomes mission. Need becomes abundance. Ability becomes talent. And then it becomes almost ridiculously easy to achieve fulfillment in every area because all the parts are working together in the same direction.

You must align your purpose with your needs, abilities, and desires. Your purpose tells you what you *should* do. Your needs (money, shelter, clothing) dictate what you *must* do. Your abilities (skills, talents, education) dictate what you *can* do. And your desires (enjoyable work, passion) dictate what you *want* to do. Taken individually each of these areas will only point you in a general direction, but when you put them all together, you'll find it easier to set specific, practical goals. This way you'll be setting goals that help you fulfill your purpose, meet your needs, do what you love to do, and do what you're really good at.

The Power of Clarity

H.L. Hunt, a man who rose from a bankrupt cotton farmer in the 1930s to a multi-billionaire when he died in 1974, was once asked during a TV interview what advice he could give to others who wanted to be financially successful. He said only two things are required. First, you must decide exactly what it is you want to accomplish. Most people never do that in their entire lives. And secondly, you must determine what price you'll have to pay to get it, and then resolve to pay that price.

Clear Goals Are Essential

Clear goals and objectives are essential to the success of any business, and this is no less true of building your own career. If you don't take the time to get really clear about exactly what it is you're trying to accomplish, then you're forever doomed to spend your life achieving the goals of those who do. In the absence of a clear direction for your life, you will either meander aimlessly or you will build a career that you don't feel good about. You may make some money, and you may do some interesting work, but the end result will not resemble anything you ever made a conscious decision to build, and ultimately you will be left with the sinking feeling that maybe you took a wrong turn somewhere along the way. Do you ever look at your career and think to yourself, "How on earth did I get here?"

If setting goals is so critically important, then why is it that so few people take the time to define exactly where they want to go? Part of the reason is a lack of knowledge about how to set clear goals. You can go through years of schooling and never receive any instruction on goal setting at all. A failure to understand the immense importance of establishing clear goals is also common. But those who truly know what they want often outperform everyone else by an enormous degree.

A frequent deterrent to goal setting is the fear of making a mistake. Teddy Roosevelt once said, "In any moment of decision, the best thing you can do is the right thing, the next best thing is the wrong thing, and the worst thing you can do is nothing." Setting virtually any goal at all is better than drifting aimlessly with no clear direction. The best way I know to guarantee failure is to avoid making clear, committed decisions. Every day is already a mistake if you don't know where you're going. You're probably spending most of your time working to achieve other people's goals. The local fast food restaurant, TV advertisers, and the stockholders of the businesses you patronize are all very happy for that. If you don't decide what you really want, then you've decided to hand your future over to the whims of others, and that's always a mistake. By taking hold of the reins yourself and deciding where you'd like to go, you gain a tremendous sense of control that most people never experience in their entire lives.

Many people assume that because they have a direction, they must therefore have goals, but this is not the case and merely creates the illusion of progress. "Making more money" and "building a business" are not goals. A goal is a specific, clearly defined, measurable state. An example of the difference between a direction and a goal is the difference between the compass direction of northeast and the top of the Eiffel Tower in France. One is merely a direction; the other is a definite location.

Define Goals in Binary Terms

One critical aspect of goals is that they must be defined in binary terms. At any point in time, if I were to ask you if you had achieved your goal yet, you must be able to give me a definitive "yes" or "no" answer; "maybe" is not an option. You cannot say with absolute certainty if you've fully completed the outcome of "making more money," but you can give me a definitive binary answer as to whether or not you are currently standing on top of the Eiffel Tower. An example of a clear business goal would be that your gross income for the month of April this year is $5000 or more. That is something you can calculate precisely, and at the end of the month, you can give a definitive answer as to whether or not your goal has been achieved. That is the level of clarity you need in order to form a goal that your mind can lock onto and move towards rapidly.

Be Detailed

Be as detailed as possible when setting goals. Give specific numbers, dates, and times. Make sure that each of your goals is measurable. Either you achieved it, or you didn't. Define your goals as if you already know what's going to happen. It's been said that the best way to predict the future is to create it.

Commit Goals to Writing

Goals must be in writing in the form of positive, present-tense, personal affirmations. A goal that is not committed to writing is just a fantasy. Set goals for what you want, not for what you don't want. Your subconscious mind can lock onto a clearly defined goal only if the goal is defined in positive terms. If you put your focus on what you don't want instead of what you do, you're likely to attract exactly what it is you're trying to avoid. Phrase your goals as if they are already achieved. Instead of saying, "I will earn $100,000 this year," phrase it in the present tense: "I earn $100,000 this year." If you phrase your goals in future terms, you are sending a message to your subconscious mind to forever keep that outcome in the future, just beyond your grasp. Avoid wishy-washy words like "probably," "should," "could," "would," "might," or "may" when forming your goals. Such words foster doubt as to whether you can really achieve what you are after. And finally, make your goals personal. You cannot set goals for other people, such as, "A publisher will publish my software by the end of the year." Phrase it like this instead: "I sign a North American retail publishing contract this year that earns me at least $100,000 by the end of the year."

Objectify Subjective Goals

What if you need to set subjective goals, such as improving your own level of self-discipline? How do you phrase such goals in binary terms? To solve this problem, I use a rating scale of 1 to 10. For instance, if you want to improve your self-discipline, ask yourself on a scale of 1 to 10, how do you rate your current level of self-discipline? Then set a goal to achieve a certain specific rating by a certain date. This allows you to measure your progress and know with a high degree of certainty whether or not you've actually achieved your goal.

Goal Setting Is an Activity

Setting clear goals is not a passive act. It doesn't happen automatically. You must take direct conscious action in order to make it so. Everything counts, and nothing is neutral. You are either moving towards your goals, or you're moving away from them. If you do nothing or if you act without clarity, then you are almost certainly a victim of "being outgoaled." In other words you are spending your time working on other people's goals without even knowing it. You are happily working to enrich your landlord, other businesses, advertisers, stockholders, etc. Each day you spend working without a sense of clarity about where you're headed is a step backwards for you. If you don't actively tend your garden, then weeds will grow automatically. Weeds don't need to be watered or fertilized. They just grow by themselves in the absence of an attentive gardener. Similarly, in the absence of conscious and directed action on your part, your work and your life will automatically become full of weeds. You don't need to do anything at all to make this happen. And when you finally get around to taking a serious look at where you are and where you want to go, the first thing you'll have to do is pull out all those weeds.

Reading this article will do absolutely nothing for you unless you turn it into some form of physical action. The best thinking unfortunately gives you zero results. In reality, you won't even be paid a penny for your thoughts. You can have the most creative idea in the world, but ideas themselves are utterly worthless. You only get results from the physical actions you take, never for the ideas you have. In order to get any kind of tangible results at all, you must act on an idea. You must communicate it, build it, implement it, and make it real.

Clarity Is a Choice

If you've been running your career in an unfocused manner, just waking up each morning and seeing what happens, then it is absolutely crucial that you take the time to decide and write down exactly where it is you want to go. How much longer will you continue to climb the ladder of success, only to realize too late that it was leaning against the wrong building? Just pick a point in the future, whether it's six months from now or five years from now, and spend a few hours writing out a clear description of where you want to be at that time. I know many people who aren't sure where they want to go, so they avoid committing anything to writing in order to "keep their options open." What would happen if you pursued that attitude to its logical conclusion? If you always kept your options open and never made any firm commitments, then you'd never get promoted, start your own business, get married, have a family, move to that new home, etc. except to the degree that someone else made that decision for you.

I used to have a friend like this, who still hasn't decided what he wants to do with his life. He yields control of his life to others without even realizing it, simply because he's unwilling to take the time to define a vision for his own life out of fear of making the wrong choice. His life is ruled by others who push their goals onto him, which he accepts by default. Ask yourself if you're in the same boat. If a friend of yours became totally committed to getting you to change something in your life at random — your career, your living situation, your relationship, etc. — could s/he do it just by being absolutely certain and committed that it's the right thing for you? Could a business associate come along and radically alter your plans for the week without you ever deciding consciously that such a change is consistent with your goals? We all suffer from problems like these to the degree that we fail to set clear goals for ourselves. There is a big difference between recognizing and acting on a true opportunity and being knocked off course without making a conscious decision to shift gears.

Waiting for something to inspire you and hoping that the perfect outcome will just fall into your lap is nothing but a fantasy. Clear decision making doesn't happen passively; you actually have to physically put in the time to make it happen. If you don't have clear goals simply because you don't know what you want, then sit down and actively decide what you want. That sense of knowing what you want isn't going to just come to you in a form of divine inspiration. Clarity is a choice, not an accident or a gift. Clarity doesn't come to you — you have to go to it. Not setting goals is the same thing as deciding to be a slave to the goals of others.

Clear Goals Sharpen Present-Moment Decisions

Your reality will not match your vision exactly. That's not the point. The point is for your vision to allow you to make clear daily decisions that keep you moving in the direction of your goals. When a commercial airliner flies from one city to another, it is off course over 90% of the time, but it keeps measuring its progress and adjusting its heading again and again. Goal setting works the same way. Maintain a clear list of goals not because that's actually where you'll end up but because it will give you tremendous certainty in deciding what you need to do today. When someone contacts you with an "opportunity" out of the blue, you'll know whether it's a real opportunity or a waste of time. The long view sharpens the short view.

As you begin moving towards your goals, you'll gain new knowledge along the way, and you'll have to adapt your plans as you go. You may also change your vision if you get partway there and decide it's not quite what you really want. Ill-formed goals are still far superior to no goals at all.

I was once told by someone that I should end each day by crossing it off my calendar and saying out loud, "There goes another day of my life, never to return again." Try this for yourself, and notice how much it sharpens your focus. When you end a day with the feeling that you would have lived it the same if you had the chance to repeat it, you gain a sense of gratitude that helps you focus on what's really important to you. When you end the day with a feeling of regret or loss, you gain the awareness to try a different approach the next day.

You'll see a measurable difference in your life the very first day you establish clear, committed goals, even if your first few attempts aren't perfect. You'll be able to make decisions much more rapidly because you'll see how they'll either move you towards or away from your goals. On the eve of his death, Walt Disney had a reporter crawl into bed with him so he could share his vision for Disney World, six years before its completion. When Disney World finally opened, another reporter commented to Walt's brother, Roy, "It's too bad Walt did not live to see this." Roy replied, "Walt saw it first. That's why we are seeing it now." Clear goals allow you to achieve the first half of H.L. Hunt's success formula. By deciding exactly what you want to accomplish, committing it to writing, and reviewing it on a daily basis, you bring your goals into reality with the power of your focus.

Chapter 6

Quarterly Planning

Today I finished typing up my detailed plan for this quarter, which is about 10 pages long. I revise my goals and plans roughly every 90 days, and I find that although this can be tedious (usually 10–15 hours of tiresome work), it's an essential tool for me, not just for running a business but for managing my entire life. Life can get pretty complicated sometimes, and it's easy to get knocked off track by external pressures if you don't know precisely where you're headed. When you're working for several days on a particular project, and a new opportunity comes along in a totally different area, it can be tough to make a clear decision if you aren't able to mentally pull your mind out of that project and see the forest for the trees. Having a written plan you can review at any time makes it easy to review your current situation from a bird's eye view, so you can make more consistent decisions.

In the previous chapter, I explained my approach to setting goals and planning, But another thing I include in my planning document is a list of assumptions that I made in putting the plan together. These are often assumptions about what I expect to happen, such as how long I think it will take to complete a particular project. Invariably I'll get a few weeks into my plan, and I'll hit a snag. So I go back to my list of assumptions and look for any that may have turned out to be wrong. Then I can adjust those assumptions and update the plan accordingly. But if I find that all the assumptions still seem to be accurate, then I usually feel safe that the heart of the high-level plan is still OK — I may just need to alter the way I'm currently implementing it. Just today I had to turn down two potential licensing deals; on the surface they looked potentially lucrative, but in light of my overall long-term goals, it's clear they would be off course for me.

When you create a 90-day plan, you're really looking ahead much further than just 90 days. I typically think ahead at least two years to figure out what I should be doing over the next 90 days. There are many decisions that look good when you consider them on a 3–6 month time frame, but when you look 2+ years ahead, they seem more problematic. It's a lot like AI chess programs — the computer player will think a particular move is optimal when it looks ahead 5 ply, but when it looks ahead 10 ply, it ends up picking an entirely different move. So it is when making short-term plans. You'll create the best plans if you look ahead a few years and think about where you'll end up, and then use that long time perspective to decide what you need to be doing right now. And for certain big decisions, like whether you'd like to have another child, you may want to look ahead much further. The long view sharpens the short view.

When I was single and living alone and hadn't yet started my own business, this kind of detailed planning would probably have been overkill. But now that my life is much more complicated, it helps me cut through the possible quagmire of confusion and really focus. The more complicated my life gets, the more important I find it to spend time clarifying my goals and plans.

The main thing a written plan does for me is gives me a sense of peace, knowing that I've thought everything through consciously, and everything is covered. It can be hard to make choices such as . . . should I spend time with the wife and kids, or exercise, or practice my next speech, or write an article, or work on my book, or do some marketing tasks, or play poker, or read a book? One thing I've learned is that I tend to do a bad job making these kinds of balancing decisions on the spur of the moment — I vastly underrepresent some areas while overworking others, so something important slips through the cracks. I just don't have the time to think several years ahead when making every single decision. It's only by creating a high-level plan that I can trust that I'm able to achieve the right balance and get the really important things done while consciously deciding what areas can afford less attention. I can trust the plan because I know I spent the time thinking things through to create it, so it acts as a tool that helps me simplify and speed up daily decisions.

Once you have a solid written plan, the next trick is to learn how to work it effectively. I manage my daily workflow using a system based on the one in David Allen's excellent *Getting Things Done* book.

Questions about Planning

I've received some questions from readers wanting to know more about planning. I'll try to address them here.

Planning is such hard work. And it's hard to keep plans up to date. So why do it?

The best advice I can give here is to try it both ways and see for yourself. Although it would be best to do this over a reasonably long period of time, such as 90 days, you can do a simple experiment in just a couple days. One day, don't create a plan for your day, and just see what happens — live and work as you normally would. If you want, you can even use yesterday for this first part. But the night before the second day, set aside about 30 minutes to set clear goals for your next day (three interesting goals is a good number), and plan out the details of those goals to create a to do list. Then write up a schedule for your day — not just your workday, but the entire day from when you wake up until when you go to sleep. Aim for a challenging day but one you think you can still do; push yourself a bit, but keep it achievable. Think about what you would consider the absolute best use of that day. And do this planning work alone, quietly, and with no distractions. Then live that day according to your written plan to the best of your ability.

Then after living through day one and day two, you decide which you like better. You can take notes about what you experienced at the end of each day, or you can just go by feel; maybe rate each day on a scale of 1 to 10. Think about where you'll be in a year if you experience 365 day ones vs. 365 day twos. Note that there isn't a prescribed right or wrong answer here. The choice depends on your personal values.

What you're likely to experience on day two is that things don't go quite according to plan. That's common. But even though it probably didn't go according to plan perfectly, how well did it go compared to day one? Were the results better or worse? And was it worth the extra 30 or so minutes to create the plan?

Now, if you don't want to take a whole day to do this, I'll give you a shorter version. Set aside two 2-hour blocks of time during your day today. It doesn't matter when they occur, but it would be best if they are times when your energy level is about equal and the level of interruptions you'll experience is roughly the same. If you can't get equivalent 2-hour blocks on the same day, then use the same time period on two separate days. For the first 2-hour block, just do what you'd normally do during that time period. That's your control. In fact, if you want to make it the previous two hours you've just experienced, that would probably be fine too. But for the second two-hour block, spend the first 15 minutes making a detailed to do list of everything you want to get done in that block, and then schedule the remaining 1:45 at least to the granularity of 15-minute increments. Then follow your plan. See which time block you like better.

Yes, it's hard to keep plans up to date, but the plan itself isn't as important as the habit of planning. It's the idea of using a vision of the future to sharpen your present-moment decisions that is the real key to planning. The benefit of a written plan is that it allows you to instantly refresh that vision of the future at any time just by reading it.

What's the connection between planning and visualization?

I see planning as a tool for visualization instead of vice versa. Planning allows you to mentally create a model of your future. And a written plan allows you to keep that model consistent. Every plan is inaccurate to some degree because we don't really know how the future will turn out. And the future is purely a mental construct — an illusion — because you never exist in the future, only in the present. So planning and visualization don't create the future. All they can do is affect your present. But by using a consistent, internally congruent vision of the future to make decisions day after day, you start to build momentum, and you'll ultimately achieve your goals.

I don't create plans now, and I don't have a problem achieving my goals most of the time. Planning seems overkill. So why bother with it?

If you don't have any really big goals, you don't need a plan. But then, you're probably selling yourself short in your goal-setting. For example, if you have a job and set a goal to increase your income by 10% this year, and you pretty much expect that to happen if you just continue working as you always have been, then why would you need a detailed written plan for that? You wouldn't. But that's a rather impotent goal, isn't it?

Now what if you set an ambitious goal to increase your income by 100% this year? And you see that it's virtually impossible for that to happen passively at your present job. Now you've got to pull the ol' brain out of the cobwebs and do some thinking. This is a situation where you have to think about where you want to be a year from now to know what you need to do during the next 30 or 90 days. It's probably not at all clear what the first step should be. Chances are good that there is a way to achieve this goal, but the path to get there isn't obvious. This goal will require you to be proactive and consistent in your actions; you can't just passively coast your way to an ambitious goal like this one.

Now imagine the above scenario. . . . what if after about

15 hours of work, you could produce a written step-by-step plan showing you exactly what you need to do to increase your income by 100% over the next year? It tells you very clearly what you must begin doing this very week in order to get started. And the plan makes sense to you — it won't be easy, but it's pretty clear that if you follow it, you probably will achieve your goal. Would those 15 hours be a worthwhile investment?

On the other hand, what is likely to happen if you try to increase your income by 100% , and you don't have a plan to get there, but you still try to make the best choices you can? Most likely you'll be a lot more hesitant and uncertain in your decision making, and that will likely lead you to procrastinate. Should you try to work towards a big promotion within your company? Look for a new job? Quit and start your own business full-time? Begin building a part-time business while keeping your day job? Try doing consulting work on the side? You'll never feel too confident about any of these choices until and unless you can paint yourself a clear mental picture of where each path will lead you.

Fuzzy thinking leads to hesitancy in acting. Clear thinking makes it easier to act boldly and consistently. And really ambitious goals generally require bold and consistent action.

So if you feel you don't really need to plan, chances are you're not setting very challenging goals to begin with, and you probably aren't stretching yourself much. And if that's how you want to live, that's perfectly fine, but then why are you reading this? Why not take on something a bit more ambitious? Set a goal to double your income in a year . . . or write your own book and get it published . . . or spend a month in a country you've never been to . . . or quit smoking and lose 50 pounds . . . whatever truly inspires you.

One nice thing is that for many goals, there are already pre-made plans to get you there. For example, if you want to run a marathon, there are pre-planned six-month training programs you can follow, such that if you just follow them blindly each day, you will gradually build up the needed level of endurance, and you'll be able to at least finish the 26.2 miles on race day. It doesn't mean that pre-made plans are any easier to follow than the ones you make yourself from scratch, but using other people's plans can definitely save you some time.

I tried to create written plans once, but my plans never worked out. So I just sort of gave up on that whole concept. Am I just broken?

You're not broken. Planning is very, very difficult to do well. It's a skill like any other that takes tremendous patience and practice to learn. If you sit down and create a plan, and it doesn't work, then don't use that setback as a reason to blame planning itself. Rather consider that you simply need to continue to build your skill at planning and/or execution. Being able to set an ambitious goal, create a plan to achieve it, and then work the plan all the way to victory is a skill that can take a lifetime to master.

How do you actually create a plan? What tools do you use?

I've tried many different planning and "life management" tools over the years, and I have some strong opinions about some of them. I'm sure many people will disagree with me, and that's fine. This is entirely my personal opinion regarding my own experiences.

MS Outlook—Piece o' crap. The slogan for this software should be, "By Golgafrinchans, for Golgafrinchans." I know some people love this software. I'm not one of them. Outlook's biggest problem is its inflexibility. You're stuck with using a particular paradigm for planning and scheduling. I am just way too left-handed to stomach this program for more than a week. And if you don't know what a Golgafrinchan is, then I'm sad to say that you probably are one.

Franklin Planner—Piece o' crap, both in paper and software versions. Again, the problem is inflexibility. You have to buy into the Franklin model of reality. That's a great model for some projects but a lousy model for others.

OPA Life Planner—Utter crap. This software is based around Tony Robbins' Outcome-Purpose-Action (OPA) planning model, later renamed to Rapid Planning Method (RPM). The paradigm lacks flexibility, and the software is bug-ridden and amateurish.

Palm or other PDAs—Golgafrinchan heaven. Even as this technology has improved a lot since I first bought my Palm IIIxe a few years ago (which now sits in a closet), most of the handheld organizing software is barely worth a mention. Puny screens, inflexibility, and tedious interfaces (pen and paper is often faster) make this a poor overall choice. I prefer thinking outside the box, and this is a very small box.

Pen and Paper—One of my all-time favorites. It's cheap, reasonably fast, readily available, and incredibly flexible. Try drawing a mind-map on a PDA, or look at your schedule, to do list, and quarterly plan simultaneously on its tiny screen. You can spread out multiple sheets of paper and quickly move from one page to another — massive surface area. Software has tried hard to duplicate the flexibility of paper, but paper is still better and faster for certain things. Of course a major drawback to paper is that it's tedious to edit and update, and I'm sure you can think of other problems with paper as well. *Regular Text Editor*—Not bad. It's not quite as flexible as paper but still much more flexible than dedicated planning tools. You can use any planning paradigm you want, and you can switch paradigms without having to switch software. You can use different paradigms for different pieces of your plan — top-down, bottom-up — it's your choice.

Action Outline is my overall favorite piece of software that I use for high-level planning. You can learn more about it here: https://www.actionoutline.com/

I use it every single day. On the surface it doesn't really look like a planning tool. The program works like a combination of Windows Explorer and MS-Word. On the left side of the screen, you have an expandable directory-like structure. And on the right side of the screen, there's a regular text editing window. So what this program allows you to do is to create pieces of text (about anything you wish) and organize them into a hierarchical structure. And then you can expand and collapse pieces of that structure however you wish, looking at your overall plans from a high-level or drilling down into the details of any particular section. What I like most about this program is that it takes care of managing a hierarchical structure for you, but it doesn't force you to use any particular planning paradigm. You could use it merely as a text editor and type up your entire plan in a single file. Or you could develop an entire plan in a collapsible outline form and not even use the text editor part of the program. Or you can use a combination of both. So as I try different methods of planning, I find that this software can always adapt. I've used it one way to create a 90-day plan for my life, another way to outline a book, and still another way to write a speech. And most of all, the program is extremely fast, and it's very quick to switch from one part of a plan to another. I recommend downloading the free trial to see if you like it, and there are other outlining programs you can find on the net, but this one is my personal favorite.

What individual documents do you create to manage your time, and how do you use them?

Calendar—First I have a yearly paper calendar, one page per month. I buy one at Office Depot each year for $5–10. A paper calendar works fine for me because my schedule isn't filled with pre-scheduled appointments, so very little of my work has to be done one a particular day and time. If I had a lot of time-bound appointments though, I probably would use something more sophisticated. I don't use this calendar for scheduling my day; it's only used for recording stuff that must happen on a particular day. For example, this coming week I can see that I have a Toastmasters meeting on Weds, a meeting with my financial planner on Thurs, and a speech contest on Saturday. That's it for my appointments for the week.

   Values List and Mission Statement—I maintain a list of my values as seen at the bottom of the About page of my website, along with my personal mission statement:

   https: //stevepavlina.com/about/

   Whenever I have to make really big long-term decisions, I consult these to make those decisions. They're both maintained in Action Outline, so I can bring them up with a hotkey at any time.

Goals List—This is a list of all my long-term goals (everything 90-days away or longer). Some of these will take me at least a decade to accomplish. The goals are all sorted into categories (physical, social, career, financial, etc). This list is also maintained in Action Outline. I look at this list at least once a week, and I update it every 1–2 weeks.

Projects List—This is a list of all the projects I have, maintained in Action Outline. To create this list I chop my big goals into individual projects that can be measured and achieved. For example, if one goal is to make a certain amount of money, then a project would define what I have to do to earn it. These projects are sorted in order of priority, and I often add notes below each project title to brainstorm a few ideas for each one. So if I get an idea out of the blue for an inactive project, I can type up those ideas quickly and get back to work on my current project.

90-Day Plan—This is my plan of what I need to do over the next 90 days. I review it every single day and update it weekly. And once each quarter I totally rewrite it.

30-Day Goals and Plans—This doc contains my short-term goals and plans for what I intend to do over the next 30 days, maintained in Action Outline. I review and update it at least once a week. The purpose of this document is to take the first 30 days of my 90-day plan and break it down to a finer level of granularity. There's a lot of back-and-forth reworking between this doc and the 90-day plan.

30-Day Schedule—Now I take my 30-day goals and plans and break them down week by week and day by day. While I maintain a 30-day schedule, I only plan 1–2 weeks in advance. So here I'm taking my 30-day goals and breaking them down even finer into individual action steps. Then I decide which days I'll complete those actions. I don't use a calendar for this. I just use a linear list of days in Action Outline, so it's really fast and easy to edit (click and drag tasks around), and I can see what I have scheduled for many days ahead. I also pull the appointments from my paper calendar and insert them into the days in my 30-day schedule. I find this method of scheduling to be the most efficient I've tried so far. This is also done in Action Outline, so I can pull up my schedule with a keypress at any time and add/remove items whenever I want. The paper calendar is mainly for long-term scheduling beyond 30-days; otherwise, I don't need the paper calendar for short-term scheduling. This schedule just involves assigning tasks to days; it doesn't get any more granular than that. I update this doc every day.

Daily To Do List and Schedule—At the end of each day, I look at the previous doc to see what I have to do on the coming day. Then in my work journal (a paper spiral notebook), I make a to do list that includes all the goal-oriented tasks I need to do the next day, and I also add any spontaneous tasks that may have come up in the past 24 hours, like returning phone calls. This list includes both personal and business tasks as well as any appointments. After I create the to do list for the next day, I create an hour by hour schedule for the day. I like to work in 2-hour chunks, so I basically chop my days up into several of these chunks with breaks or meals between each chunk, and then I assign tasks from my to do list to each chunk. Now I can see what tomorrow will look like and how it will turn out. It usually takes me 10–15 minutes to create my to do list and schedule for the next day. And at the same time, I'll often edit my 30-day schedule. It's rare that a particular day goes exactly according to plan — this happens only about 20% of the time.

Usually I get more or less done than I had planned. But that's OK; I still get more done with a plan than without one.

Inbox—This is a plastic tray on top of my desk. Any piece of paper coming into my office must first go into the inbox, including mail, business cards, notes from conferences, etc. Then once every few days, I process all the info in my inbox into my system, turning it into goals, projects, actions, or just filing it for reference. As I write this, my inbox contains to-do items from my last Toastmasters meeting, notes from a 3-hour microbiology/health lecture I attended on Thursday, and a business article I want to scan for ideas.

Outbox—This is a plastic tray below my inbox tray. It's for anything that needs to leave my office, like mail to drop off. It's empty most of the time.

Filing Cabinet—A 4-drawer filing cabinet sits within arms reach, so I use this for storing anything I might want to keep for reference. Items that enter my office through my inbox will usually either end up here, in the trash, or in my outbox.

Hopefully the above will give you a good picture of how I manage my time. I like this particular system and find it works very smoothly for me, and I'm always continuing to evolve it. Since most of the info is stored in Action Outline, I can bring up these docs with a hotkey, and there's no time lost for the program to load because it's always running in the system tray with all the text ready for viewing at all times, much faster than using a word processor. And I can switch between these different docs with a single mouse click. I probably bring up Action Outline about a dozen times per day on average.

Chapter 7

Transitioning to a Purpose-Driven Life

Once you've defined your purpose and identified some goals and projects based on that purpose, most likely you'll find that you'll have to move in a very different direction. You may have been trekking down your current path for years, and now you've set a whole new direction. It's possible that almost every part of your life will have to change — your health habits, social relationships, work/career, and even your spiritual practices.

Having gone through such a transition myself multiple times (usually by conscious decision), I have some advice to share about making such a transition you may find helpful.

Shifting Gears

Clarity is greatly reduced whenever you turn a corner in life, so the first thing you can expect when you change directions is that you'll experience a tremendous lack of clarity. Imagine you're driving a car through a busy downtown area. You may be able to clearly see the road for many blocks ahead of you. But if you're about to make a turn, you may not be able to see more than a few yards around the corner as you approach it. Your view is blocked by obstacles, and if it's a road you've never been down before, you won't quite know what to expect. However, once you've completed most of the turn, you will again be able to see very far down the road in your new direction.

Life is much the same way. Your ability to see what lies ahead will be very limited as you shift directions, but as you complete the turn, clarity will once again return.

I experienced this when I shifted my career last year from full-time software publishing to full-time writing and speaking. Before I committed to the transition, I had only a fuzzy notion of what the new career would be like. No matter how much planning I did, it was still fuzzy — there were simply too many variables I couldn't predict. I was out of my element. As I began to transition, almost every week I had to rethink my plans — long-term planning was impossible because I was constantly learning new things that would corrupt my old plans. I had to live one day at a time through much of it. But after a few months, I was able to get my bearings and could see the road ahead of me very clearly. Then I was able to again set long-term goals with confidence.

Take Your Time

When you make a big transition in your life, take your time. You don't have to change every area of your life simultaneously within the next 30 days. Changing too many things at once can be stressful, so take steps to manage the stress by keeping some parts of your life stable as you change others. If you turn a corner too fast, you'll flip your car or spin out of control. But even if you take the turn gradually, you'll still feel a force pulling you to the side. You have to maintain your grip on the wheel and keep control as you change directions. Once you've completed the turn, then you can relax and loosen up a bit — your new momentum will carry you forward.

During the past two years, my wife and I had a second child, we moved our family and businesses from Los Angeles to Las Vegas (with all the side-effects of moving to a new state), I began a whole new career, and we bought a new house earlier this year. My local social circle has changed completely — most of the people I spend the most time with now are people I didn't even know two years ago. And then there's all the personal development work I did, which caused me to experience many personal changes during this time, including changes in long-term habits.

This was a lot of change, and if we tried to do it all at once, it would have been overwhelming. But by splitting it up and spreading it out over many months, it became manageable. After our son was born and while we moved to Vegas, we kept our careers and incomes stable. Then we took a few months to get settled into our new city (new preschool for our daughter, exploring the city). Once we had a stable routine going, then I began building new skills and developing a local social network, and a few months later, I made the career switch full-time. During that time my wife kept her career and income stable, while mine was unstable. Now over the next year my work and my income are likely to change even more, so I'm keeping the other parts of my life relatively stable.

Usually I'm operating outside my comfort zone in at least one area of my life (but not all areas), and I find that the more I do this, the more simultaneous change I'm able to tolerate.

Preparing Your Environment for Change

One easy step you can take in beginning your transition is to prepare your environment to help reinforce your new goals. Most likely your environment reflects your current identity, so if you want to change your identity, you can start by changing your environment. For example, one of the first things I did when transitioning from software to speaking was to reorganize my office. I asked myself, "What kind of office would a professional speaker/writer have, and how would it be different from that of a software developer?" I made a list of changes and then implemented them quickly. I removed all my game programming books, packed up my shareware awards, packed up all the games, etc. I reorganized my filing cabinet with empty file folders for future speeches and cleared some shelf space for new books. This created a void to be filled with the trappings of my new career.

I did this clearing process about a year ago, and now that void is filled. My files are full of past speeches and reference material. My bookshelf holds new books on speaking, writing, and personal development. I have a shelf with a half-dozen speech contest trophies and plaques. So every time I walk into my office, it reinforces my identity as a speaker/writer.

Dealing With Social Resistance

Aside from the *things* in your environment, you also have to deal with the *people*. Many readers have told me that social resistance is a big problem for them. They make a plan to change their lives, and then their friends or family talk them out of it.

You need to trust your own judgment more than the opinions of others. Even if you turn out to be wrong, you'll learn more about yourself in the process and will be able to make better decisions in the future.

Many people fear change, and your attempt to change your life for the better is perceived as a threat. Ask yourself which of your friends will be able to handle the new you once you've completed the transition? Will you still be able to be friends after the change? Close, genuine friendships can handle such a transition. But many casual friendships and associations cannot.

The same goes for other relationships. Many relationships do not survive such a change. But what kind of relationship did you have anyway if making a change to better your life results in a breakup? It just means the relationship was based on something impermanent. You're better off making the change and seeing if your relationship is strong enough to handle it than using the relationship as an excuse for staying put. A good relationship should help you grow, not hold you back, and there's nothing wrong with temporary relationships. A breakup is not the end of the world. People do it every day and live to talk about it.

When I transitioned to building a personal development business, a lot of casual friendships were broken. It's probably no surprise that many people in the gaming industry don't respect the field of personal development, even though they often invest enormous time in improving their technical skills (which I see as a form of personal development). Such people reacted to my change as if it was a personal affront. I expected this though, so it didn't slow me down. I went through the same thing when I first started my games business.

When you make a big change in your life, you can expect social resistance regardless of the nature of the change. Social resistance is ubiquitous– don't take it as a sign that you're doing anything wrong. Use your own intelligence to figure out if you're on the right path. No matter how right your decision is, there will be people to tell you you're wrong and that you're making a big mistake. Just allow those people to be upset, and be on your merry way. Don't take it personally. Most of all, don't argue with them — you're just wasting your breath. Focus on taking action, and let them adjust if they can.

I believe the best way to confront social resistance is by counteracting it with social harmony. Get involved with a new social group that will mitigate the effects of your old group. Develop new friendships in harmony with your new self-image. I recommend you do this as early as possible, before you break off any old relationships that can't handle the transition. Start spending more time with your new reference group than your old one. Your new group will help pull you in the direction you want to go, which will automatically loosen the bonds with your old group. You'll naturally enjoy spending more time with people who are encouraging you and less time with those who are discouraging you.

For me this involved joining Toastmasters, which is an organization devoted to personal growth, communication, and leadership skills. Over a period of several months, I built a new social circle starting with a single Toastmasters club and gradually branching outward, and my old reference group gradually faded as I spent less and less time in their midst.

A few old friendships were able to endure this transition with me. Some people that knew me for years as a game developer were able to accept my new identity, so we still keep in touch, but the nature of these friendships has changed. I think the best friendships are those that can stand the test of time, where the friendship is based more on who you are than on what you do or what you have.

For *Deep Space Nine* fans, say you're friends with Curzon Dax. Could you still be friends with Jadzia or Ezri? It depends on the nature of the friendship.

Are Your Friends an Elevator or a Cage?

Let's explore the role of the people in your life. Are they elevating you to be the best person you can be, or are they holding you back?

I mentioned in my last entry that when going through major life shifts, like changing careers, I would shift the people with whom I spent the most time. We've all gone through periods where the people in our lives have changed — graduation, moving to a new city, getting a new job, joining a new club, etc. I don't think I need to convince you just how much influence other people can have over your identity. If you've ever experienced a major shift in your people environment, then you know that you change as well.

Most people don't make these choices consciously though. You might consciously decide to spend more time with a certain friend, or you may ask someone out on a date to begin a new relationship. But few people choose the bulk of their existing friendships deliberately. Chance meetings may be out of your control, but the strength or weakness of your existing connections is largely under your control.

Think for a moment about the 5–10 people with whom you spend the most time. Even include online communities if you spend a lot of time reading them — which individuals are having the most influence over your thinking right now? Actually write out the list — it should only take a minute. And this includes family members.

Now look at the list. It's been said that this list will give you a glimpse into your future.

Do you want to become more like these people? Yes or no. Is anyone on the list a bad influence that causes you to backslide? Is anyone on the list a shining light that encourages you to reach new heights?

Now have you ever thought about consciously changing this list? Do you realize that you have the ability to populate this list by choice instead of by chance? You're free to say no to having certain people in your life, and you're also free to make the effort to introduce new people you want in your life. Sometimes there are serious consequences, such as with family members and bosses, but it's still a choice.

There's no "getting rid of people." People are always drifting in and out of each others' lives. Associations grow into friendships, and friendships fade into associations. You don't get rid of anyone. The truth is that in order to make room for new people and new experiences, you may need to loosen up some of your existing connections.

What about loyalty? Shouldn't you always be loyal to your

friends? Once you have a close friend, even if their influence on you is somewhat destructive, shouldn't you stick by them? Loyalty is one of my personal values. But my value of loyalty means being loyal to my vision of my highest and best self and to my core values. And this runs both ways. While I know I can't afford to hang on to friendships that conflict with my values, I also can't hang onto friends that I may be holding back in some way. I only want to have win-win relationships where everyone benefits.

Loyalty to a friend sometimes means having to let go. It means being loyal to their highest and best self as well. If someone is destroying their health by smoking, for example, you aren't showing loyalty by smoking right along with them. What are you being loyal to then? Death? True loyalty sometimes requires that you break destructive connections, get yourself back on solid ground, and then decide what you can really do to help your friend (which sometimes requires letting them hit bottom).

How about a realistic example? Back when I was in college, I would occasionally use pirated software. I had several friends who were software pirates and who'd keep offering it to me, and I'd sometimes accept if it was something I wanted. But when I started my own software business after graduation and began thinking about the kind of person I wanted to be, I realized that software piracy had to go. So I decided to stop.

But of course what happened next? You guessed it. Some more pirated software was offered to me, and I gave into the temptation. And then I beat myself up about it. And that pattern cycled a few more times until . . .

I realized if I wanted to stop using pirated software, I had to stop associating with pirates. So I consciously decided to let those relationships fade, which on a couple occasions required actively telling the other person I couldn't have them in my life anymore (and why). Then I built closer friendships with more honest people who would never consider software piracy. My new friends and associates elevated my thinking to their level, and I found it easy to let go of software piracy permanently. I was positively infected by the thoughts of those who don't pirate software, so my new mindset just doesn't even consider piracy. I either buy what I want, or I do without.

Today I use a lot of shareware programs, and they're all registered. Even though I could save money by tracking down pirated versions, I just don't. I won't even consider it. And it has nothing to do with being worried about getting caught or getting a computer virus or not having the latest version or wasting too much time. Software piracy just isn't me. I'm a non-pirate.

This change had some unexpected positive side effects too. When I let go of piracy, I felt a lot more deserving of my successes. It elevated my sense of self. There was nothing on my computer to give me the subconscious message: yeah that was a nice success, but you're still a thief. This is one very basic example of how consciously changing the people in your life can change you for the better.

What about trying to change/rescue people in need? Although I don't think it's impossible to transform a destructive relationship from within, it's very difficult unless you have a lot of support. While you're trying to elevate the other person, you're sinking at the same time. You'd probably need a buffer of many other strong relationships in order to transform one destructive relationship. I think the best approach is to leave the destructive relationship behind, form new relationships to get your strength back, and then (keeping those new relationships), you'll have the ability to revisit and transform the old destructive relationship with a much reduced risk of being sucked back into old patterns.

I think you can get a pretty good idea of what a person is like by looking at the people who surround that person. Think about it for a moment. What kind of people does the U.S. president spend the most time with? What about the Dalai Lama? Your children? Even Jesus was surrounded by the 12 Apostles. So one betrayed him, and one thrice denied knowing him, but 10 out of 12 isn't bad. If you had a dozen loyal devotees following you everywhere, perhaps you might enjoy some fairly elevated thinking too.

It can take a lot of courage to tell someone, "I'm sorry, but I can't have you in my life anymore." But even though this might seem like a selfish act at times, it's often the best thing for the other person too. If a relationship is holding you back in some way, understand that it's also hurting the other person. For example, if you work for an abusive boss, your acceptance of that situation constitutes silent approval, encouraging your boss to continue to behave abusively (towards yourself and others).

If you smoke and suddenly say to all your smoker friends, "I'm sorry, but I can't continue to be friends with people who smoke anymore. I've decided I need to be a nonsmoker," you'll probably meet with a lot of resistance. But if you follow through with it, your actions will eat away at some of those old friends. And a year later when you're a nonsmoker, one of them will contact you privately, "I'd like to quit too. Can you help me?" And you will be able to help. You might even renew your old friendship, but at a whole new level.

The kinds of relationships I seek out today are those which

have the potential to be win-win, where both people can help each other to grow in positive ways without holding each other back. Not one person using the other — synergy. I'm always open and inviting of new friendships of this kind. If I ever feel like I'm stuck in a cage, I know it's time to reach out and make some new connections and/or loosen up some old ones.

When you consciously undergo a major life transition, be patient with yourself. When you meet with environmental or social resistance, take steps to reduce or minimize the resistance instead of struggling against it. Expect that clarity will be reduced as you turn the corner, but know that it will return as you're speeding off in a new direction. Managing a major life transition is a lot of work, but you'll come out the other side in a much better position. The long-term gain is well-worth the short-term pain.

Chapter 8

Conscious Evolution

In this final chapter in the *Meaning of Life,* I'll attempt to present a broader view of why personal development is so important and why I believe that investing in your own growth is the best investment you can make.

Conscious Evolution

When I used the word "evolution" to describe my world view, I was not using the word in the biological sense of natural selection, breeding, and mutation. A few people seemed to get stuck on that term. I was using the broader definition of evolution: a process in which something passes by degrees to a different stage, especially a more advanced or mature stage.

This includes the evolution of thought, society, knowledge, and the capabilities of life — the evolution of the noosphere moreso than of the biosphere. The noosphere is our collective knowledge and wisdom, and today it "evolves" far faster than any biological entities. In fact, the ongoing biological evolution of human beings is so slow as to be virtually irrelevant compared to the rate at which the noosphere is evolving.

Our biology has evolved little in the past 1000 years, but our technology, knowledge, and culture have evolved massively.

So when I said I wanted to serve the process of evolution, I did not mean it in the biological sense — biological evolution is too slow and has become largely irrelevant. If the biological evolution of humans does continue, it is likely to occur by choice, not as a result of ongoing breeding and mutation over eons. But what matters most right now is the evolution of the noosphere.

What About The Biosphere Though?

I agree that the planet is in bad shape environmentally. But we can't afford to wait for biological evolution to fix these problems. If we do that, humans will almost certainly become extinct before we have the chance to evolve into something better. Some experts assert that the environment is in such bad shape that we won't make it to the end of this century . . . that the destructive processes we've put in motion may already be irreversible, even if we we were to immediately start doing everything we could to correct them.

Ignoring these problems isn't a viable option, but I also think that attacking these problems directly is doomed to failure. There are already people doing that now, but they seem to be making little progress. They may slow the rate of decay a bit, but they're nowhere near reversing it. There's too much resistance, and by the time the resistance can be effectively overcome, we'll be way past the point of no return.

Consider something as simple as diet. The environmental consequences of the Standard American Diet are severe — to say it wastes resources and pollutes the environment is a gross understatement. The U.S. government subsidizes most of it, which hides the true costs. It takes 18 times as much land to grow the food for someone eating the SAD diet compared to someone eating a vegan-plant based diet. If someone eating the SAD diet were to eat vegan for just one day, they'd save more water than they would by not showering for a year. Your decision to eat a burger for dinner is not merely a health choice — it's an environmental and political one as well. In fact, virtually anything you might do environmentally or politically in your lifetime is irrelevant compared to the simple decision of what to eat each day. You could devote your entire life to Greenpeace, and it will only amount to a puny fraction of what you'd accomplish by living as a resource-guzzling playboy who happens to be vegetarian.

And yet, so few people are aware of the long-range consequences of what they do because their "knowledge" is fed to them by marketers. They buy into the social context instead of thinking for themselves. People make billions off the SAD diet, and it doesn't hurt them financially if you want to plant a few trees on the side or clean up some trash to feel good about yourself, as long as you keep downing the burgers. But try to attack the diet that makes them rich, and they'll drown you in marketing until you submit.

I could write about this stuff all day, but it's already been written. The average person will simply avoid it, and to the degree it does get read, it will only be resisted or ignored. People must have the wherewithal to seek it out because they really want to know what's going on. But so few people currently have the courage and discipline to do that.

I don't see the solution as spending more time and energy attacking such problems directly. If I attempt that, I'll only be outmarketed by those with a massive financial stake in perpetuating the current belief system, however false it may be. I could spend my whole life attacking smoking, for instance, but in the end it won't make much difference — I might convince a fair number of people to quit, but many more will become smokers, and many who do quit will simply adopt a substitute vice. So overall there won't be much impact. My resistance will simply be met with stronger resistance. Force will fail.

So What's the Solution?

The best solution I can think of is to work on human awareness itself, to help more people see the benefits and navigate the obstacles in pursuing their own conscious growth. I don't think this requires a change in our biology but rather a shift in the noosphere. I think we already have the biological capabilities necessary to fix the problems of this planet if they're fixable at all, but we currently lack the awareness, discipline, and courage as a species to step up and take personal responsibility for doing what is right. Most people would rather live an illusion than spend time thinking about the best possible contribution they could make with their lives. But I think I can help change that. A good number of people seem to be reaching similar conclusions.

I figure that over the course of my lifetime, the absolute best thing I can do is to implant and strengthen the seed of conscious personal growth into the noosphere, in cooperation with other people who have similar missions.

Human beings have so much untapped capacity it's ridiculous. If we can edge up the realization of this capacity and raise the average level of awareness of human beings, then more people will "wake up" and start living with greater consciousness and courage. They'll begin to drop destructive habits and adopt more positive ones. They'll start to define a meaningful purpose for their lives, and along the way they'll encourage others to do the same. They'll stop living in fear of their own shadow and obsessing over trivialities. And these "upgraded" human beings, living more consciously and courageously, will have a far better chance of solving the greatest problems of humanity and of successfully managing the greatest risks that threaten us.

My mission then is to encourage and assist people in pursuing their conscious growth, to help them find a path away from a life of quiet desperation and towards a life of courage, purpose, and responsibility. I have not been able to think of any better contribution I could make with my life than this.

For me this mission is deeply intertwined with the pursuit of my own personal growth. By working on myself, I increase my capacity to help others. And by helping others to become more conscious and conscientious, I build an environment that reinforces my own growth and which helps to insulate me from the forces that threaten to suck me back down into low-awareness living.

Right now I'm manifesting this mission in the form of articles, blog entries, and an upcoming book. Over the next decade I expect to extend it across a variety of different media: articles, books, audio programs, speeches, seminars, etc. Beyond that I envision putting together a formal organization of some kind to help people grow more consciously and to upgrade their courage, discipline, and awareness, and also to serve as an outlet for people who wish to team up with others who have similar missions.

One challenge is figuring out how to live within the current noosphere while working to change it. You have to rely on the current economic system to provide for your basic needs. My solution thus far has been to systematize and automate my income as much as possible, so I have the freedom to pursue higher level projects without having to invest too much time and energy in making a living. I have a few other ideas that should improve that situation even more.

I don't really see the solving of social/global problems as the primary end though. I think that's mainly a side effect of the pursuit of growth, not the purpose of growth itself. I see the pursuit of greater courage, consciousness, and conscience as an end in itself. However, such pursuits will solve many problems along the way, and often this is easier than attacking such problems directly. For example, you can attack problems like being overweight, being addicted to smoking, and having unsatisfying relationships and make very little progress across the board. But if you work on developing your courage, awareness, and self-discipline, these problems will solve themselves — in fact, they'll become almost trivially easy.

Investing in your own growth is the best investment you can make. Don't think for a minute that it's a selfish pursuit. Quite the contrary — it is in fact the best thing you can do to help others. If you feel you are not contributing much with your life right now, don't beat yourself up about it or deny what you could become if you were only strong enough. Instead, turn inward and work on yourself until you become the kind of person on the inside who automatically expresses good as a manifestation of who you are.

Conquer your fear, and the rest is easy.